THE SINGLE VEGAN

'Full of delicious and quickly prepared dinners' — *The Vegan*

THE SINGLE VEGAN

Simple, convenient and appetizing meals for one

by
Leah Leneman

Thorsons
An Imprint of HarperCollins*Publishers*

Thorsons
An Imprint of GraftonBooks
A Division of HarperCollins*Publishers*
77-85 Fulham Palace Road,
Hammersmith, London W6 8JB

Published by Thorsons 1989
5 7 9 10 8 6

A CIP catalogue record for this book
is available from the British Library

ISBN 0 7225 1454 9

Typesetting by MJL Limited,
Hitchin, Hertfordshire
Printed in Great Britain by
Woolnough Bookbinding Limited,
Irthlingborough, Northamptonshire

Contents

Introduction

Most cookery books, vegan or otherwise, are aimed at a family of four, and dividing ingredients to make them suitable for one is often not feasible. Of course, the same dish could be eaten four nights running, but who wants to do that? Or you could freeze the remainder, but only certain types of dishes are suitable for freezing, and it still means eating leftovers. Also, many of the recipes found in ordinary cookery books involve a degree of time and effort which may be appropriate for the preparation of a meal for a family, a partner or friends, but does not seem worth the bother when cooking just for oneself.

It is not just the amount of time needed to cook a meal that counts either; the planning involved is often the most off-putting thing. Yet to stick to the same tried and true recipes day after day is very boring indeed — no wonder so many companies are now producing convenience meals for one person! Some of them aren't bad at all, but they rarely match up to a home-cooked meal, and they are *much* more expensive.

This book is designed to overcome those obstacles to cooking for one. Each week begins with a Sunday lunch. Dinner on Sunday night is slightly more time-consuming than on other nights of the week, as this is likely to be the one day of the week when some extra time can be afforded. And for this meal a dessert recipe is also provided. From Monday to Friday the assumption is that lunch will be had out. The recipes for evening meals are all quick and easy to prepare, while at the same time providing lots of variety. For Saturday a lunch recipe is given, but the likelihood is that one night a week a break from cooking will be desired, and a meal had at a restaurant or with friends. By the end of any week all perishable ingredients will have been used up, and, to make the planning as simple as possible, a shopping list precedes each week's menus.

The book does not, however, have to be utilized in the way described above; it can be used in the same way as any other cookery book, since each recipe stands on its own. Nor does it have to be used for single people only; ingredients are far more easily doubled, or even quadrupled, than halved or quartered. And although the recipes are all vegan — for even vegans not living alone may have to prepare separate meals for themselves — the menus aim to be interesting and varied enough to satisfy vegans, lacto-vegetarians and omnivores.

Breakfast

Given the importance of starting the day with something nourishing, one can't really *not* mention breakfast, although no recipes are provided. Vegans have plenty of choice these days with dairy-free mueslis and the like (however, some cereals are not suitable because they are fortified with an animal-derived vitamin D). Porridge is a nice starter for a cold winter's morning; or for a savoury hot breakfast, scrambled tofu, or thinly sliced and fried tofu, fits the bill nicely. Breakfast is one meal that causes no problems to single vegans.

Lunch

As indicated in the introduction above, the assumption is that the majority of people using this book will not be concerned with preparing a daily lunch. Every vegetarian restaurant now caters for vegans, and even non-vegetarian restaurants often have vegan salads and/or baked potatoes, etc. Eating lunch out in many parts of the country is no longer a problem for a vegan.

If daily restaurant lunches are not easily affordable then it is easy enough to bring a packed lunch in to work. There are an increasing number of vegan pâtés and spreads for sandwiches, as well as vegan biscuits. A number of the Saturday and Sunday lunch dishes in this book — such as spreads, salads and the like — could be taken to work for midday lunches as well.

For those who do not go out to work but lunch at home, the weekend lunch recipes could be used. A healthy alternative is simply a daily mixed salad, with differing ingredients and accompaniments for variety. There are also many more packet soups and convenience foods like tofu burgers which are vegan these days.

There are some people who prefer to eat a large midday meal and only a light supper in the evening; the daily recipes could of course be used for a midday meal and the above suggestions be utilized for the evening meal.

Quantities

The most useful kitchen implement for a single person is a dieter's scale: using one of those you can weigh as little as ¼ oz (5g), which is invaluable for small quantities. I often weigh liquids in the same way — i.e., instead of trying to measure ⅛ pint (70 mls/⅓ cup) in a measuring cup I just put an ordinary teacup on the scale and pour in 2½ oz (70g) in weight of the liquid.

Many cookery books insist that imperial and metric measurements should not be mixed. As far as I am concerned, anyone using this book should feel free to mix imperial, metric and even American measurements to their heart's content.

Vegetables

Life is much easier for single people buying vegetables these days, now that so many greengrocers and supermarkets are self-service. You used to have to buy at least ½ pound of anything instead of just the odd vegetable you actually wanted. Some people may still feel a bit self-conscious about buying just one or two small inexpensive items; the easiest way round this is simply to use the same shop(s) regularly, since if you are known to be a regular customer you are less likely to be looked at askance if buying only a single carrot and single onion one day.

Recipes in standard cookery books often call for 1 onion or 2 onions, which is a bit meaningless since one can buy onions as small as 2 oz (55g) or as large as 8 oz (225g). When I specify a 'small onion' I mean 2-4 oz (55-115g). It is usually quite easy to find onions of this size, but if your local shop only has large ones you can chop off this amount, wrap the remainder in clingfilm and store it in a fridge until onion is required for another recipe. Garlic cloves are also very variable in size; if the only kind available seems large enough to flavour a dish for four people then this too can be quartered with the remainder wrapped in clingfilm and stored in the fridge (though it's a good idea to put an extra plastic bag round it to keep the fridge from reeking of garlic). When a recipe calls for a small carrot I mean 2-3 oz (55-85g); a small green pepper is about 6 oz (170g), a small courgette (zucchini) 3-4 oz (85-115g).

Certain vegetables are more awkward for one person to use, for example cauliflower. I have tried always to incorporate such vegetables into more than one recipe in a week's menu so that you are not left with a large chunk of it in the fridge with no idea what to do with it. Celery is a particular nuisance I find because a little of it goes very nicely in some dishes but a whole head is difficult to use up. Spring onions (scallions) are arguably in the same category except that they will keep in the fridge for some weeks.

I know that some single people prefer to keep a stock of frozen vegetables, but I can't see the point when it is easier (and a lot cheaper) to buy half a dozen fresh Brussels sprouts than to pull out the same number of frozen ones. The only exception I make is green beans or peas when they are out of season.

Pulses

Many of the recipes in this book call for tinned (canned) beans. The reason is simply that unless you have a pressure cooker, cooking dried beans takes an awfully long time, which may be acceptable if you are cooking for a family but not for a single person. Unlike vegetables, which lose vitamins (not to mention flavour) when tinned, protein is not lost in the canning process, so tinned beans are as nutritious as freshly cooked ones. Admittedly they can be high in salt content, and some British brands add sugar as well, but it is easy enough to rinse the beans off before using them. There is no doubt, however, that tinned beans work out a lot more expensive than dried ones, so if money is more important than time then by all means use home-cooked beans instead of tinned ones: a small tin or half a large one is equivalent to 2 oz (55g) dried beans, and an ordinary tin to about 4 oz (115g).

Butter beans and red kidney beans are available in small tins, which obviates the need to use the other half of a tin later in the week. All other beans are available only in larger tins so I have used them in two recipes in the relevant week. The beans not used in the first recipe should not be left in the tin but transferred to a jar and refrigerated until required.

Certain pulses — e.g., lentils, aduki beans, split peas, and black-eyed peas — are not readily available in tins and are quite quick to cook so in those cases the dried varieties are called for.

Salads

There are basically two types of salad. (Well, three if you count the typical British salad of limp lettuce leaves, a slice of tomato and one of cucumber, topped with something sliced, with vinegary salad cream over it, but anyone reading this book is unlikely to think of such a thing when talking of salads.) The first kind of real salad is a meal in itself. Such salads feature as recipes for some weekend lunches.

The second kind is a side salad, i.e., it accompanies a dish in the same way as cooked vegetables. Many of the recipes in this book would be nice accompanied by a salad even when this is not specified. It is easy enough to make a salad for one person. Some lettuce or cress, a small grated carrot, a few sliced button mushrooms — that alone makes a very palatable salad even if there is nothing else to add to it, and if there is celery, a few spring onions, green pepper or other leftovers in the fridge, so much the better. A few chopped black olives really zing up a salad. The easiest dressing for this type of salad is a little oil — especially virgin olive oil — mixed with a little cider vinegar or lemon juice, perhaps with a pinch of mustard, and any additional seasoning desired. It is useful to have a ready-made vinaigrette dressing handy, but unfortunately most supermarket ones are made with malt vinegar which is anything but nutritious (or even *nice*). Fortunately, more wholefood shops are beginning to stock good ones.

Herbs and Spices

It has become easier to obtain fresh herbs of late, and some people grow their own. Obviously fresh herbs have a wonderful flavour, and anyone who has access to them will certainly want to use them, but the majority will find it much easier to keep a variety of dried herbs in stock. When herbs are called for in recipes it is dried herbs that are meant.

As far as spices are concerned, although there is nothing intrinsically wrong with the mixture of spices which go to make up 'curry powder', far more interesting variations of flavour can be obtained by using the spices themselves. For the best flavour, coriander and cumin seeds are much better bought whole and ground in a small pestle and mortar when required. I realize such a suggestion may seem surprising in a book which is aimed at simple and quick recipes, but the average time required to grind a teaspoonful of spice cannot be more than about five seconds, and it is especially beneficial when cooking for one simply because these spices are likely to be stored for a long time, since only a little is required for any one dish, and if bought already powdered then much of the flavour will gradually be lost.

Rice and Pasta

If used straight from the packet, brown rice generally takes about 45 minutes to cook, which makes it less than ideal for a really quick meal. However, if it is covered with boiling water in the morning and left to soak all day then it will only take about 20-25 minutes. (The method is to drain the soaking water, cover the rice with water about a ¼-inch (5mm) over the top and a little salt, bring to the boil, lower heat, cover pan and simmer until all the water is absorbed.) This is all very well for well-organized people but rather annoying if you arrive home in the evening to realize you have forgotten the soaking step. There are now several brands of brown rice available in supermarkets which require no soaking and take only 25 minutes or so to cook. The method with these types of rice is different: the rice is covered with lots of boiling water and simmered uncovered before being drained and more hot water poured over it. As the water is not all absorbed, this type of rice is not suitable for pilaus and similar dishes which require the flavouring to be incorporated into the rice. These supermarket packets also work out rather more expensive than rice bought at a wholefood shop. The best compromise may be to use the latter normally but keep the supermarket kind in stock for emergencies or when the soaking has been forgotten. I find about 3 oz (85g) wholefood shop brown rice or 2½ oz (70g) supermarket brown rice to be right for one serving.

Wholemeal (whole wheat) pasta is available now in a variety of shapes and sizes. Not all of the packets provide information on cooking time. Twelve to fifteen minutes seems to be about the average time required for most types of wholemeal (whole wheat) pasta to cook.

Most Chinese noodles sold in this country are egg noodles, but Chinese shops do sell eggless noodles. There is one brand of thin noodles called 'steamed noodles' while another brand of somewhat thicker noodles is called 'vegetarian noodles'. There are also noodles made from rice flour which are egg-free. And recently wholemeal (whole wheat) Chinese-style egg-free noodles have come on the market; obviously if these are available they are preferable to white flour brands. Most Chinese noodles take only 2-3 minutes to cook, making them an ideal food for those in a hurry.

Dessert

Dessert is not a necessary part of anyone's diet, and many people are perfectly happy to end a meal with a savoury taste. Unfortunately, there are many of us brought up in such a way that a meal simply is not complete unless it ends with a sweet. For those of us in that situation all that can be done is to try and make the sweet course a healthy addition to the diet.

Fresh fruit is the most commonly suggested healthy dessert, but for die-hard sweet-toothed types, a fresh apple, pear or banana, which may be very welcome in the morning or between meals, does not constitute a real dessert. That is not to say there aren't some fresh fruits which do. In the summer months fresh strawberries, raspberries, and similar soft fruit — particularly if served with cashew or coconut cream — certainly does, also sweet melons and the like. In the winter tropical fruits like fresh pineapple or mango are definitely reserved for dessert. Another winter fruit which can be classified as a dessert is the persimmon (also called Sharon fruit). For those who have not tried this fruit, it should be eaten when it is so soft it feels almost rotten. The skin is peeled off and the inside is unbelievably sweet.

Tinned fruit is not the same, of course, but there are an increasing number of varieties tinned in juice rather than sugar syrup; served with cashew cream or custard made from soya milk, they can serve as a pleasant dessert as well.

Nowadays there are an increasing number of sweets suitable for vegans at health food stores. There are ready-made puddings by Provamel and Granose with a soya (soy) milk base; once opened these will keep for several days in the fridge so can be used by a single person on successive nights. There are now vegan ice-creams available at many health food stores and also at Jewish delicatessens and some large supermarkets.

Naturally a convenience-type dessert can never be the same as a home-made one, which is why I have included sweet recipes for one in Sunday meals, when there may be extra leisure time to make them.

Staples

A shopping list precedes each week's menus, but it is assumed that certain foods will be kept permanently in the larder, and therefore those foods do not appear on weekly shopping lists. The items considered staples are the following:

HERBS

Sage
Thyme
Marjoram
Basil (sweet basil)

Oregano
Bay leaves
Rosemary
Mint

SPICES

Nutmeg
Cinnamon
Cloves
Ginger
Turmeric
Cumin
Coriander

Mustard seeds
Chilli (chili) powder or
    cayenne pepper
Paprika
Garam masala
    (a mixture of spices)

MISCELLANEOUS

Wholemeal (whole wheat) bread
Sea salt and black pepper
Garlic salt

Baking powder
Raw cane sugar
Wholemeal (whole wheat) flour
Yeast extract
Autolized yeast flakes or Good
   Tasting Yeast*
Soya milk

Vegan margarine
Vegetable oil (e.g. soya/soy
   or corn)
Extra virgin olive oil
Soya (soy) sauce
Cider vinegar
Tomato purée (paste)
Brown rice
Wholemeal (whole wheat)
   spaghetti and macaroni

*Good Tasting Yeast comes as flakes or powder and has a delicious 'cheesy' taste. It can be ordered from The Good-Tasting Food Company, PO Box 188, Summertown, TN 38483, USA. I understand that autolized yeast flakes, available in the UK, are similar, but I cannot attest to this as I order the above-mentioned kind.

Spring/Summer Recipes

Week 1

SHOPPING LIST

Vegetables and Fruit

Spring onions (scallions)
Olives
1 small red pepper
1 lb (455g) potatoes
6 small onions
10 oz (285g) mushrooms
Capers
Spring cabbage (collards)
4 oz (115g) apricots
Garlic
1 small green pepper
1 small leek
1 small courgette (zucchini)
4 oz (115g) green beans

Miscellaneous

10 oz (285g) packet smoked tofu
Red lentils
Vegetable suet or hard vegetable fat
Apple juice
15½ oz (440g) tin (can) borlotti
  (pinto) beans
Bulgur wheat
Soya (soy) yogurt
Millet
Flaked (slivered) almonds
Walnut pieces

Check that you have all the staples listed on page 13.

SUNDAY LUNCH

Italian Pasta Salad

Imperial (Metric)

3 oz (85g) wholemeal macaroni or
  other pasta shape
1 spring onion
4 olives
½ small red pepper
1 slice wholemeal bread
2 oz (55g) smoked tofu
1½ tablespoons olive oil
1 teaspoon cider vinegar
Pinch garlic salt
Pinch oregano
Freshly ground black pepper

American

3 ounces whole wheat macaroni or
  other pasta shape
1 scallion
4 olives
½ small red pepper
1 slice whole wheat bread
¼ cup smoked tofu
1½ tablespoons olive oil
1 teaspoon cider vinegar
Pinch garlic salt
Pinch oregano
Freshly ground black pepper

1. Cook the pasta until just tender. Drain, cool, then chill.
2. Mince the spring onion (scallion) and olives. Chop the red pepper. Toast the bread, then dice it. Dice the tofu. Place all these ingredients in a bowl with the cooked pasta.
3. In a cup mix the oil, vinegar, garlic salt, oregano and pepper to taste. Pour the dressing over the salad and mix it all thoroughly.

SUNDAY DINNER

Potato and Lentil Bake

Imperial (Metric)	American
½ lb (225g) potatoes*	½ pound potatoes*
2 oz (55g) red lentils	⅓ cup red lentils
4 fl oz (115ml) water	½ cup water
1 tablespoon vegan margarine	1 tablespoon vegan margarine
1 small onion	1 small onion
2 oz (55g) mushrooms	1 cup mushrooms
1½ tablespoons wholemeal flour	1½ tablespoons whole wheat flour
1 tablespoon tomato purée	1 tablespoon tomato paste
¼ pint (140ml) soya milk	⅔ cup soymilk
¼ teaspoon basil	¼ teaspoon sweet basil
Freshly ground black pepper	Freshly ground black pepper
Spring cabbage	Collards

1. Scrub the potatoes and cook them in lightly salted water until tender.
2. Cover the lentils with the water, add a little sea salt if desired, bring to the boil, lower heat and cook until the lentils are tender and water is absorbed.
3. Melt the margarine in a pan. Chop the onion and add it to the pan. Sauté for a minute or two. Slice the mushrooms and add them to the pan. Sauté for a further 3-4 minutes.
4. Add the flour and tomato purée (paste) to the pan, and stir well. Very slowly, add the milk, stirring constantly to avoid lumps. When it is boiling and thickened stir in the basil and pepper to taste.
5. When the lentils are cooked, stir them into the sauce.
6. When the potatoes are cooked (if too hot to handle, rinse them under cold water), slice them thickly. Spread them out in an oven dish, and top with the sauce. Bake at 400°F (200°C)/Gas Mark 6 for 15-20 minutes. Serve accompanied by lightly-steamed spring cabbage (collards).

*If preparing the whole week's menus, cook 1 lb (455g) potatoes and store half in the refrigerator.

SUNDAY DESSERT

Apricot Brown Betty

Imperial (Metric)	American
4 oz (115g) apricots	¼ pound apricots
1 tablespoon raw cane sugar plus additional to taste	1 tablespoon raw cane sugar plus additional to taste
1 tablespoon water	1 tablespoon water
1½ oz (45g) wholemeal breadcrumbs	⅔ cup whole wheat breadcrumbs
½ oz (15g) vegetable suet or hard vegetable fat	1 tablespoon vegetable suet or hard vegetable fat
¼ teaspoon cinnamon	¼ teaspoon cinnamon

1. Chop the apricots and put them in a small pan with sugar to taste (depending on ripeness of the fruit and personal preference) and the water, and stew until tender.
2. Put the breadcrumbs in a bowl. Grate the vegetable fat and add it to the breadcrumbs. Add 1 tablespoon sugar and cinnamon as well and mix thoroughly.
3. Place half the breadcrumb mixture at the bottom of a small greased oven dish, spoon the apricots on top and then the remainder of the breadcrumb mixture.
4. Bake at 400°F (200°C)/Gas Mark 6 for about half an hour. Serve with cashew or coconut cream if desired.

MONDAY

Smoky Beans

Imperial (Metric)	American
1 small onion	1 small onion
1 small clove garlic	1 small clove garlic
1 tablespoon vegetable oil	1 tablespoon vegetable oil
2 oz (55g) smoked tofu	¼ cup smoked tofu
3 fl oz (85ml) apple juice	⅓ cup apple juice
1 teaspoon tomato purée	1 teaspoon tomato paste
Pinch marjoram	Pinch marjoram
1 small or ½ large bay leaf	1 small or ½ large bay leaf
½ × 15½ oz (440g) tin borlotti beans	½ × 15½ ounce can pinto beans
½ lb (225g) cooked potatoes	½ pound cooked potatoes
1-2 tablespoons soya milk	1-2 tablespoons soymilk
1 tablespoon vegan margarine	1 tablespoon vegan margarine
Sea salt and freshly ground black pepper to taste	Sea salt and freshly ground black pepper to taste

1. Chop the onion. Mince the garlic. Heat the oil in a pan and add the onion and garlic. Sauté for 2-3 minutes
2. Dice the tofu. Add to the pan and sauté for a further 2-3 minutes.
3. Add the juice, purée (paste), marjoram and bay leaf. Bring to the boil, then lower heat and simmer, uncovered, for about 5 minutes.
4. Add the drained beans and cook for a further 5 minutes.
5. Meanwhile, mash the potatoes in a bowl. Heat the milk and margarine in a small saucepan and add to the potatoes, along with seasoning to taste. Spoon the mashed potatoes into a heatproof dish and place under the grill (broiler) until thoroughly heated.
6. Remove the bay leaf from the bean mixture and spoon over the mashed potatoes.

TUESDAY

Smoked Tofu à la King

Imperial (Metric)	American
2 oz (55g) mushrooms	1 cup mushrooms
½ small red pepper	½ small red pepper
6 oz (170g) smoked tofu	¾ cup smoked tofu
2 tablespoons vegan margarine	2 tablespoons vegan margarine
1 tablespoon wholemeal flour	1 tablespoon whole wheat flour
¼ pint (140ml) soya milk	⅔ cup soymilk
Sea salt and freshly ground black pepper to taste	Sea salt and freshly ground black pepper to taste
3 slices wholemeal toast	3 slices whole wheat toast

1. Chop the mushrooms and red pepper. Dice the tofu. Heat half the margarine in a frying pan (skillet) and sauté these ingredients for a few minutes.
2. Meanwhile, heat the rest of the margarine in a saucepan and stir in the flour. Gradually pour in the milk, stirring constantly to avoid lumps. Bring to the boil, then simmer for a minute or two to thicken. Season to taste.
3. Add the tofu mixture to the sauce and mix well. Cook for a minute or two, then pile onto the toast.

WEDNESDAY

Spaghetti with Bean and Caper Sauce

Imperial (Metric)

3 oz (85g) wholemeal spaghetti
1 small onion
½ small green pepper
1 small clove garlic
1 tablespoon olive oil
6 capers
1 tablespoon tomato purée
3-4 fl oz (85-115ml) water
½ teaspoon oregano
½ × 15½ oz (440g) tin borlotti beans
Freshly ground black pepper

American

3 ounces whole wheat spaghetti
1 small onion
½ small green pepper
1 small clove garlic
1 tablespoon olive oil
6 capers
1 tablespoon tomato paste
⅓-½ cup water
½ teaspoon oregano
½ × 15½ ounce can pinto beans
Freshly ground black pepper

1. Cook the spaghetti in boiling salted water until just tender.
2. Chop the onion, green pepper and garlic finely. Heat the oil in a pan and sauté the vegetables for 3-4 minutes.
3. Mince the capers. Add them to the saucepan, along with the tomato purée (paste), water and oregano. Bring to the boil, then lower heat and simmer, uncovered, for about 5 minutes.
4. Drain and rinse the beans and add them to the pan with a little black pepper. Cook until the beans are thoroughly heated. Serve over the cooked drained spaghetti.

THURSDAY

Creamy Curried Mushrooms with Bulgur Wheat

Imperial (Metric)

2½ oz (70g) bulgur wheat
8 fl oz (225ml) water
1 small onion
1 tablespoon vegan margarine
4 oz (115g) mushrooms
¼ teaspoon coriander
¼ teaspoon cumin
¼ teaspoon turmeric
¼ teaspoon powdered ginger
⅛ teaspoon chili powder
1 tablespoon wholemeal flour
½-⅔ cup plain soy yogurt
Sea salt to taste
½ teaspoon paprika

American

⅓ cup plus 1 tablespoon bulgur
 wheat
1 cup water
1 small onion
1 tablespoon vegan margarine
2 cups mushrooms
¼ teaspoon coriander
¼ teaspoon cumin
¼ teaspoon turmeric
¼ teaspoon powdered ginger
⅛ teaspoon chili powder
1 tablespoon whole wheat flour
½ – ⅔ cup plain soy yogurt
Sea salt to taste
½ teaspoon paprika

1. Put the bulgur wheat in a small saucepan, cover with the water (and a little sea salt), bring to the boil, then lower heat, cover and simmer until the water is absorbed, which only takes about 10 minutes at most.
2. Chop the onion. Heat the margarine in a frying pan (skillet) and fry the onion until just beginning to brown. Slice the mushrooms and add them to the pan. Lower heat and cook for about 3 minutes.
3. Grind the coriander and cumin if using whole seeds. Add the spices to the mushrooms and onions, and cook for 2-3 minutes longer, stirring occasionally.
4. In a small bowl, add the flour to the yogurt and stir well. Remove the mushroom mixture from the heat and stir in the yogurt. Add salt to taste.
5. Spoon the bulgur wheat into a small fairly shallow ovenproof dish and spoon the mushroom mixture on top. Sprinkle with the paprika. Place under the grill (broiler) at medium heat and leave it there for about 5 minutes before transferring it onto a plate.

FRIDAY

Millet Pilaf

Imperial (Metric)	American
1 small onion	1 small onion
4 teaspoons vegetable oil	4 teaspoons vegetable oil
2 oz (55g) millet	¼ cup millet
Sea salt to taste	Sea salt to taste
¼ pint (140ml) water	⅔ cup water
2 oz (55g) flaked almonds	½ cup slivered almonds
1 small leek	1 small leek
1 small courgette	1 small zucchini
2 oz (55g) mushrooms	1 cup mushrooms
Freshly ground black pepper	Freshly ground black pepper
¼ teaspoon ground cinnamon	¼ teaspoon ground cinnamon

1. Chop the onion. Heat 2 teaspoons of the oil in a saucepan and add the onion. Sauté for about 3 minutes until tender but not brown. Add the millet and cook for another 2 minutes or so, stirring occasionally. Sprinkle in the salt and pour in the water. Bring to the boil, then lower heat and simmer, covered, for about 20 minutes.
2. Place the almonds under the grill (broiler) and toast until lightly browned, turning frequently. Set aside.
3. Chop the leek and courgette (zucchini) finely. Heat the remaining 2 teaspoons oil in a frying pan (skillet) or wok and add the vegetables. Stir-fry for about 3 minutes.
4. Slice the mushrooms thinly and add them to the leek and courgette (zucchini). Stir-fry for a further 2-3 minutes.
5. When the millet is tender and the water absorbed, stir in the vegetables, pepper to taste, and the cinnamon. Cook for a couple of minutes longer, stirring, then remove from heat, and stir in almonds.

SATURDAY LUNCH

Green Bean Salad

Imperial (Metric)	*American*
4 oz (115g) green beans	¼ pound green beans
1 small onion	1 small onion
4 teaspoons olive oil	4 teaspoons olive oil
½ small green pepper	½ small green pepper
1 teaspoon cider vinegar	1 teaspoon cider vinegar
Sea salt and freshly ground black pepper to taste	Sea salt and freshly ground black pepper to taste
1 oz (30g) walnut pieces	3 tablespoons English walnut pieces

1. Top and tail the beans and chop them into fairly small pieces. Steam until crisp-tender.
2. Chop the onion finely. Heat 2 teaspoons of the oil in a frying pan (skillet) and fry the onion until lightly browned.
3. Chop the green pepper finely. In a bowl, combine the green pepper, beans and onion with the remaining 2 teaspoons of oil, the vinegar, and seasoning. Chill thoroughly.
4. Toast the walnut pieces under a grill (broiler) until lightly coloured. Cool. Just before eating the salad, mix the nuts into it. Accompany the salad with a slice of wholemeal (whole wheat) bread if desired.

Week 2

SHOPPING LIST

Vegetables and Fruit

1 red pepper
1 small tomato
4 oz (115g) green beans
4 oz (115g) peas (about ½ lb (225g)/
  before shelling)
3 small carrots
4 small onions
Garlic
Fresh ginger (root)
Fresh strawberries
10 oz (285g)/5 cups mung
  beansprouts
Chinese cabbage or spring cabbage
  (collards)
Lemon
1 small green pepper
4 oz (115g)/2 cups mushrooms
Mixed salad ingredients
Spring onions (scallions)
¼ cucumber

Miscellaneous

Flaked (slivered) almonds
Soya (soy) yogurt
10 oz (285g) tofu
Peanut butter
Wholemeal (whole wheat) or spinach
  noodles
Whole almonds
Sesame seeds
15½ oz (440g) tin (can)
  chick peas (garbanzo beans)
Tabasco sauce

Check that you have all the staples listed on page 13

SUNDAY LUNCH

Basque Salad

Imperial (Metric)	American
1 red pepper	1 red pepper
1 small tomato	1 small tomato
1½ tablespoons olive oil	1½ tablespoons olive oil
2 teaspoons cider vinegar	2 teaspoons cider vinegar
½ teaspoon tomato purée	½ teaspoon tomato paste
½ teaspoon paprika	½ teaspoon paprika
¼ teaspoon garlic salt	¼ teaspoon garlic salt
Freshly ground black pepper	Freshly ground black pepper
2 or 3 slices wholemeal toast	2 or 3 slices whole wheat toast

1. Cut the pepper into quarters, removing the seeds and pith while doing so.
2. Place the quarters, skin side facing upwards, under a hot grill (broiler) until the skin is blistered and blackened; move the quarters around once or twice if necessary to ensure evenness.
3. Cool slightly, then place the quarters under cold running water, and peel off the skins. Slice into thin strips and chill.
4. Scald, skin, and slice the tomato thinly.
5. In a small bowl mix together the oil, vinegar, tomato purée (paste), paprika, garlic salt, and pepper.
6. At lunchtime place the pepper strips and tomato slices on top of the toast, and spoon the dressing over everything.

SUNDAY DINNER

Vegetable Pilau Special

Imperial (Metric)	American
3 oz (85g) long-grain brown rice	½ cup long-grain brown rice
Sea salt to taste	Sea salt to taste
1 teaspoon turmeric	1 teaspoon turmeric
2 oz (55g) green beans	2 ounces fresh green beans
1 small carrot	1 small carrot
2 oz (55g) peas (about 4 oz/115g before shelling)	⅓ cup shelled peas
1 small onion	1 small onion
1 small clove garlic	1 small clove garlic
¼-½ inch piece fresh ginger	¼-½ inch piece ginger root
1 small tomato	1 small tomato
1 tablespoon vegan margarine	1 tablespoon vegan margarine
1 teaspoon ground coriander	1 teaspoon ground coriander
1 teaspoon ground cumin	1 teaspoon ground cumin
¼ teaspoon chilli powder (optional)	¼ teaspoon chili powder (optional)
1 teaspoon garam masala	1 teaspoon garam masala
1 oz (30g) flaked almonds	¼ cup slivered almonds

1. Cover the rice with boiling water and leave to soak for several hours. Drain, rinse, cover with water, add a little salt and the turmeric; bring to the boil, then lower heat, and cook until the water is absorbed and rice tender, about 20 minutes.
2. Meanwhile, chop the beans and carrot. Steam them — and the peas — until just tender. Drain and set aside.
3. Chop the onion. Crush the garlic. Grate the ginger finely. Chop the tomato.
4. Heat the margarine in a pan and add the onion. Sauté until beginning to brown. Add the garlic and ginger and cook for a minute longer. Lower heat and stir in the spices. Then add the tomato and cook for a minute or two longer. Remove from heat and stir in the cooked vegetables.
5. Place half the cooked rice on the bottom of a greased ovenproof dish, spoon the vegetable mixture over it, then top with the other half of the rice. Cover the dish (if it has no lid then use foil) and bake it at 350°F (180°C)/Gas Mark 4 for about half an hour.
6. Toast the almonds under a hot grill (broiler) until lightly browned. When the pilau is ready and dished up, sprinkle the almonds on top.

SUNDAY DESSERT

Strawberry 'Cheese'

Imperial (Metric)

1 × 5 oz (150g) carton natural soya
  yogurt
A few fresh strawberries
Raw cane sugar to taste

American

1 × 5 ounce carton plain soy yogurt
A few fresh strawberries
Raw cane sugar to taste

1. Spoon the yogurt carefully into a square of muslin or cheesecloth. Gather it up and
    tie it round the taps of the sink (or somewhere else convenient over a bowl) and
    leave it to drip for several hours or overnight. Spoon the result — which will be
    about 1½ oz (45g) in weight and resemble *fromage frais* in texture — into a small
    bowl and refrigerate until ready to use.
2. Mash the strawberries coarsely in a small bowl. Stir in the yogurt 'cheese' and sugar
    to taste.

MONDAY

Peanut Buttery Stir-fry

Imperial (Metric)	American
2½-3 oz (70-85g) brown rice*	½ cup brown rice*
3 oz (85g) tofu	⅓ cup tofu
4 teaspoons vegetable oil	4 teaspoons vegetable oil
1 small onion	1 small onion
1 small carrot	1 small carrot
2 oz (55g) green beans	2 ounces green beans
A few leaves Chinese or spring cabbage	A few leaves Chinese cabbage or collards
3 oz (85g) mung beansprouts	1½ cups mung beansprouts
1 small clove garlic	1 small clove garlic
¼-inch piece fresh ginger	¼-inch piece ginger root
1½ tablespoons peanut butter	1½ tablespoons peanut butter
4 tablespoons water	4 tablespoons water
2 teaspoons lemon juice	2 teaspoons lemon juice
1 tablespoon soya sauce	1 tablespoon soy sauce
2 tablespoons soya milk	2 tablespoons soymilk

1. Cook the rice until tender.
2. Dice the tofu. Heat 1 teaspoon oil in a wok or frying pan (skillet) and stir-fry the tofu until lightly browned. Remove from wok.
3. Slice the onion thinly. Slice the carrot into matchsticks. Chop the beans finely. Heat 2 teaspoons oil in the wok and stir-fry these ingredients 2-3 minutes.
4. Chop the cabbage leaves and add them to the wok along with the beansprouts. Continue stir-frying until just tender.
5. Crush the garlic. Grate the ginger finely. Heat the remaining teaspoon oil in a small saucepan and add the garlic and ginger. Cook for a minute or two, then stir in the peanut butter and then the water. Stir until smooth. (This much can be done before the vegetables start cooking; the rest should wait until they are nearly ready.) Add the lemon juice, soya (soy) sauce and milk, and stir well.
6. Return the tofu to the wok, and stir in the peanut butter sauce. Mix well and serve on top of the rice.

*If making the whole week's menus, cook double the amount of rice, cool and then refrigerate half of it.

TUESDAY

Mediterranean Noodles

Imperial (Metric)	American
1 small onion	1 small onion
½ small green pepper	½ small green pepper
1 small clove garlic	1 small clove garlic
1 tablespoon olive oil	1 tablespoon olive oil
2 oz (55g) mushrooms	1 cup mushrooms
3 fl oz (90ml) vegetable stock or water	⅓ cup vegetable stock or water
2 tablespoons tomato purée	2 tablespoons tomato paste
1 teaspoon oregano	1 teaspoon oregano
Sea salt and freshly ground black pepper to taste	Sea salt and freshly ground black pepper to taste
3-3½ oz (85-100g) wholemeal or spinach noodles	3-3½ ounces whole wheat or spinach noodles
1 teaspoon vegan margarine	1 teaspoon vegan margarine
1 tablespoon autolized yeast flakes	1 tablespoon Good Tasting Yeast flakes or powder

1. Chop the onion and green pepper finely. Crush the garlic. Heat the oil in a pan and sauté these ingredients 3-4 minutes.
2. Slice the mushrooms and add them to the pan. Cook for about 2 minutes longer.
3. Add the stock or water, tomato purée (paste), oregano and seasoning. Bring to the boil, then lower heat and leave to simmer, uncovered, for about 10 minutes.
4. Meanwhile, cook the noodles until just tender. Drain them and toss with the margarine and yeast. Transfer to a plate and pour the sauce on top.

WEDNESDAY

Vegetable Fried Rice

Imperial (Metric)	American
2½-3 oz (70-85g) brown rice	½ cup brown rice
½ oz (15g) almonds	⅛ cup almonds
1 tablespoon sesame seeds	1 tablespoon sesame seeds
1 small onion	1 small onion
1 small carrot	1 small carrot
1 tablespoon vegetable oil	1 tablespoon vegetable oil
3-4 oz (85-115g) Chinese or spring cabbage	3-4 ounces Chinese cabbage or collards
2 oz (55g) peas (about 4 oz/115g before shelling)	⅓ cup shelled peas
4 oz (115g) mung beansprouts	2 cups mung beansprouts
3 oz (85g) tofu	⅓ cup tofu
1 tablespoon soya sauce	1 tablespoon soy sauce
Freshly ground black pepper	Freshly ground black pepper

1. Cook the rice until tender or use rice cooked earlier in the week.
2. Toast the almonds and sesame seeds lightly under the grill (broiler). Set aside.
3. Chop the onion and carrot finely. Heat the oil in a wok or frying pan (skillet) and stir-fry the onion and carrot for about 2 minutes.
4. Shred the cabbage. Add it to the wok, along with the peas and beansprouts. Cover the wok and cook for about 3 minutes, uncovering it to stir it once, by which time the cabbage should have wilted.
5. Mash the tofu in a small bowl. Add it to the wok along with the rice. Mix well. Season with soya (soy) sauce and pepper to taste. Stir-fry the whole mixture until thoroughly heated.
6. Remove from heat and stir in toasted almonds and sesame seeds.

THURSDAY

Chick Pea (Garbanzo Bean) Burgers

Imperial (Metric)	American
½ tin chick peas	½ can garbanzo beans
1 spring onion	1 scallion
1 tablespoon soya yogurt	1 tablespoon soy yogurt
1 teaspoon tomato purée	1 teaspoon tomato paste
1 teaspoon soya sauce	1 teaspoon soy sauce
½ teaspoon marjoram	½ teaspoon marjoram
1 oz (30g) wholemeal breadcrumbs	½ cup whole wheat breadcrumbs
Wholemeal flour as required	Whole wheat flour as required
Vegetable oil as required	Vegetable oil as required
Mixed salad ingredients	Mixed salad ingredients

1. Drain and rinse the beans. Mash them in a bowl.
2. Mince the spring onion (scallion). Add it to the beans, along with the yogurt, purée (paste), soya (soy) sauce, marjoram and breadcrumbs. Mix well, and form into 3 burgers.
3. Spread a little flour on a plate. Turn the burgers in the flour so that they are coated on each side. Refrigerate them for about half an hour (or longer if more convenient).
4. Shallow fry the burgers in a little oil until browned on both sides. Serve with a mixed side salad.

FRIDAY

Spaghetti Stir-fry

Imperial (Metric)	American
3 oz (85g) wholemeal spaghetti	3 ounces whole wheat spaghetti
1-2 spring onions	1-2 scallions
1 small clove garlic	1 small clove garlic
½-inch piece fresh ginger	½-inch piece ginger root
4 tablespoons vegetable oil	4 teaspoons vegetable oil
4 oz (115g) tofu	½ cup tofu
½ small green pepper	½ small green pepper
2 oz (55g) mushrooms	1 cup mushrooms
3-4 oz (85-115g) fresh mung beansprouts	3-4 ounces fresh mung beansprouts
1 tablespoon soya sauce	1 tablespoon soy sauce
½-inch piece cucumber	½-inch piece cucumber

1. Cook the spaghetti until tender.
2. Chop the spring onion (scallion), garlic and ginger very finely. Heat 2 teaspoons of the oil in a wok or frying pan (skillet), and stir-fry for about 2 minutes. Dice the tofu and add it to the wok; stir-fry for another minute. Remove the tofu mixture from the wok.
3. Chop the green pepper and mushrooms. Heat the remaining 2 teaspoons of oil in the wok and stir-fry these ingredients for 1 minute. Add the beansprouts and stir-fry for another minute.
4. Return the tofu mixture to the wok, and add the cooked spaghetti as well. Sprinkle in the soya (soy) sauce, mix it all very well and stir-fry the whole thing for another minute.
5. Chop the cucumber very finely and sprinkle it over the top.

SATURDAY LUNCH

Piquant Chick Pea (Garbanzo Bean) Spread

Imperial (Metric)

½ × 15 oz (440g) tin chick peas
1 tablespoon soya yogurt
½ teaspoon ground cumin
½ teaspoon ground coriander
Few drops Tabasco sauce

American

½ × 15 ounce can garbanzo beans
1 tablespoon soy yogurt
½ teaspoon ground cumin
½ teaspoon ground coriander
Few drops Tabasco sauce

1. Drain and rinse the beans. Put them in a bowl and mash them coarsely. Stir in the yogurt, cumin, coriander and Tabasco sauce.
2. Serve in sandwiches or rolls, with lettuce or alfalfa sprouts if desired.

Week 3

SHOPPING LIST

Vegetables and Fruit

Spring onions (scallions)
1 lb (455g) potatoes (plus 1 extra)
Olives
½ lb (225g) mushrooms
Lemon
Mixed salad ingredients
¼ lb (115g) gooseberries
1 small onion
½ lb (225g) (plus 1 extra) courgettes (zucchini)
½ lb (225g) (¼ lb/115g shelled) peas
1 small leek
1 small red pepper
1 small green pepper
Garlic
Fresh ginger (root)
4-6 oz (115-170g) tomatoes

Miscellaneous

Soya (soy) yogurt
Rolled oats
10 oz (285g) packet tofu
Miso
Tahini
Peanut butter
7 oz (200g) tin (can) butter (lima) beans
Cornflour (cornstarch)

Check that you have all the staples listed on page 13

SUNDAY LUNCH

Mediterranean-style Potato Salad with Yogurt Dressing

Imperial (Metric)

½ lb (225g) potatoes*
¼ pint (140ml) soya yogurt
1 spring onion
3 olives
¼-½ teaspoon garlic salt
½ teaspoon oregano
1 tablespoon olive oil

American

½ pound potatoes*
⅔ cup soy yogurt
1 scallion
3 olives
¼-½ teaspoon garlic salt
½ teaspoon oregano
1 tablespoon olive oil

1. Cook the potatoes until tender. Cool slightly.
2. Put the yogurt in a bowl. Mince the spring onion (scallion) and olives and add them to the bowl along with the garlic salt, oregano and olive oil. Mix well.
3. Dice the potatoes and add them to the bowl. Mix them in. Cover bowl and chill thoroughly. (This is fairly substantial on its own, but crispbread, toast or toasted pitta bread provide a pleasantly contrasting texture.)

*If making the entire week's menus then cook 1 lb (455g) potatoes; cool half of them and then refrigerate for use later in the week.

37

SUNDAY DINNER

Savoury Mushroom Bake

Imperial (Metric)	American
1 oz (30g) wholemeal flour	¼ cup whole wheat flour
1 oz (30g) rolled oats	¼ cup rolled oats
¼-½ teaspoon garlic salt	¼-½ teaspoon garlic salt
1 oz (30g) vegan margarine	¼ cup vegan margarine
4 oz (115g) mushrooms	2 cups mushrooms
2 teaspoons vegetable oil	2 teaspoons vegetable oil
3 oz (85g) tofu*	⅓ cup tofu*
1 tablespoon soya yogurt*	1 tablespoon soy yogurt*
1 tablespoon water*	1 tablespoon water*
½ teaspoon miso*	½ teaspoon miso*
1 teaspoon tahini*	1 teaspoon tahini*
1 teaspoon lemon juice*	1 teaspoon lemon juice*
1 teaspoon paprika*	1 teaspoon paprika*
Mixed salad ingredients	Mixed salad ingredients

1. Mix the flour, oats and garlic salt in a bowl. Rub in the margarine finely. Put the mixture in a greased ovenproof dish and bake at 375°F (190°C)/Gas Mark 5 for about 10 minutes.
2. Slice the mushrooms. Sauté them in the oil for 3-4 minutes.
3. Put the tofu, yogurt, water, miso, tahini, lemon juice, and paprika into a liquidizer and blend thoroughly.
4. Stir the sautéed mushrooms into the tofu mixture. Spoon this on top of the flour and oat base, return to oven and bake for 20-25 minutes. Accompany the dish with a mixed salad.

*If making the whole week's menus then double the amount of each of these ingredients; spoon half of the mixture into an airtight container and refrigerate for use later in the week. Halve the remainder of the tofu (4-5 oz/115-140g) from the shopping list and put it in the freezer for Friday's recipe (page 44).

SUNDAY DESSERT

Gooseberry Dessert

Imperial (Metric)

4 oz (115g) gooseberries
¼ pint (140ml) water
Raw cane sugar to taste
½ oz (15g) semolina

American

¼ pound gooseberries
⅔ cup water
Raw cane sugar to taste
⅛ cup farina

1. Top and tail the gooseberries and place them in a saucepan. Cover them with the water and sugar. Bring to the boil, then lower heat, cover, and simmer until the gooseberries are tender.
2. Stir in the semolina (farina) carefully, and simmer for a couple of minutes longer until the mixture thickens.
3. Cool, then chill thoroughly.

MONDAY

Macaroni Stew

Imperial (Metric)	American
3 oz (85g) wholemeal macaroni (or other pasta shape)*	3 ounces whole wheat macaroni (or other pasta shape)*
1 small onion	1 small onion
1 tablespoon vegetable oil	1 tablespoon vegetable oil
1 small courgette	1 small zucchini
1 small potato	1 small potato
4 oz (115g) fresh peas (2 oz/55g shelled)	⅓ cup shelled peas
¼ pint (140ml) water	⅔ cup water
1 teaspoon yeast extract	1 teaspoon yeast extract
1 bay leaf	1 bay leaf

1. Cook the pasta until tender.
2. Chop the onion. Sauté it in the oil in a saucepan for 2-3 minutes.
3. Chop the courgette (zucchini) into thick slices. Dice the potato finely. Add these ingredients to the onion. Sauté for another minute or two, stirring.
4. Add the peas, water, yeast extract and bay leaf. Bring to the boil, then lower heat, cover pan, and simmer for 7-10 minutes.
5. Add the cooked drained pasta to the vegetables and cook for a minute or two longer. Remove the bay leaf before dishing up. (NB. This dish is easier to eat with a spoon than a fork.)

*If making the whole week's menus then cook double this amount of pasta. Cool half of it, then rinse it (to avoid stickiness), drain and refrigerate it in an airtight container for use later in the week.

TUESDAY

Butter (Lima) Bean and Vegetable Stew

Imperial (Metric)	American
2½-3 oz (70-85g) brown rice*	½ cup brown rice*
1 small leek	1 small leek
1 tablespoon vegetable oil	1 tablespoon vegetable oil
2 oz (55g) mushrooms	1 cup mushrooms
½ small red pepper	½ small red pepper
1 bay leaf	1 bay leaf
¼ pint (140ml) water or	⅔ cup water or
vegetable stock	vegetable stock
1 × 7 oz (200g) tin butter beans	1 × 7 ounce can lima beans
1 tablespoon peanut butter	1 tablespoon peanut butter
Soya sauce to taste	Soy sauce to taste

1. Cook the rice until tender.
2. Clean the leek well and chop it finely. Sauté in the oil for 2-3 minutes.
3. Slice the mushrooms. Chop the red pepper finely. Add them to the pan and sauté for a further 2 minutes. Add the bay leaf and the water or stock; bring to the boil, then lower heat, cover pan and simmer for 5-7 minutes.
4. Drain and rinse the beans.
5. Add the peanut butter to the vegetables in the pan and mix well. Add the beans, taste for seasoning, and add soya (soy) sauce. Continue simmering gently until the beans are thoroughly heated; remove bay leaf and serve over the rice.

*If making the whole week's menus then cook double this amount of rice; cool and then refrigerate half.

WEDNESDAY

Macaroni au Gratin

Imperial (Metric)	American
Tofu mixture from Sunday Dinner (page 38)	Tofu mixture from Sunday Dinner (page 38)
2 tablespoons water	2 tablespoons water
2 teaspoons tomato purée	2 teaspoons tomato paste
2 tablespoons autolized yeast flakes	2 tablespoons Good-Tasting Yeast
3 oz (85g) macaroni (or other pasta shape), cooked	3 ounces macaroni (or other pasta shape), cooked
1 oz (30g) wholemeal breadcrumbs	½ cup whole wheat breadcrumbs
1-2 teaspoons vegan margarine	1-2 teaspoons vegan margarine
Mixed salad ingredients	Mixed salad ingredients

1. If you do not have the tofu mixture already prepared then turn to page 38 for the recipe. Turn the mixture into a bowl; add the water, purée (paste) and 1 tablespoon of the yeast, and stir.
2. Add the cooked macaroni to the bowl and mix thoroughly. Turn the mixture into a greased oven dish; top with the breadcrumbs, remaining tablespoon of yeast, and margarine. Bake at 350°F (180°C)/Gas Mark 4 for about half an hour. Accompany with a mixed green salad.

THURSDAY

Indian Rice

Imperial (Metric)

1 small onion
1 small garlic clove
¼-inch piece fresh ginger
1 tablespoon vegetable oil
½ teaspoon ground cumin
¼ teaspoon ground coriander
½ teaspoon turmeric
½ teaspoon garam masala
Pinch chilli powder
4-6 oz (115-170g) tomatoes
1 small carrot
½ small red pepper
2 oz (55g) shelled peas
  (about 4 oz/115g unshelled)
2 tablespoons water
2½-3 oz (70-85g) brown rice, cooked
Sea salt to taste

American

1 small onion
1 small garlic clove
¼-inch piece ginger root
1 tablespoon vegetable oil
½ teaspoon ground cumin
¼ teaspoon ground coriander
½ teaspoon turmeric
½ teaspoon garam masala
Pinch chili powder
¼ pound tomatoes
1 small carrot
½ small red pepper
⅓ cup shelled peas
2 tablespoons water
½ cup brown rice, cooked
Sea salt to taste

1. Chop the onion finely. Mince the garlic and ginger. Heat the oil in a pan and sauté the onion, garlic and ginger for 2-3 minutes.
2. Add the spices to the pan and stir briefly.
3. Chop the tomatoes, carrot and red pepper. Add them to the saucepan along with the peas. Stir well for a minute or two. Add the water, bring to the boil then lower heat, cover pan and leave to simmer for about 5 minutes.
4. Stir in the cooked rice and add salt to taste. Continue cooking in covered pan for about 5 minutes longer, stirring once or twice, before dishing up.

FRIDAY

Tofu and Green Pepper Savoury

Imperial (Metric)	American
1 tablespoon yeast extract	1 tablespoon yeast extract
¼ pint (140ml) boiling water	⅔ cup boiling water
4-5 oz (115-140g) frozen tofu	½-⅔ cup frozen tofu
1 spring onion	1 scallion
1 small clove garlic	1 small clove garlic
1 small green pepper	1 small green pepper
2 oz (55g) mushrooms	1 cup mushrooms
2 tablespoons vegetable oil	2 tablespoons vegetable oil
½ lb (225g) potatoes, cooked	½ pound potatoes, cooked
1 tablespoon cornflour	1 tablespoon cornstarch
1 tablespoon cold water	1 tablespoon cold water
Sea salt and freshly ground black pepper to taste	Sea salt and freshly ground black pepper to taste

1. Dissolve the yeast extract in the boiling water in a bowl and add the frozen tofu pieces. Cover and leave for ten minutes until the tofu has defrosted. (If at that time the tofu still has a hard centre and the liquid has cooled off, the mixture can be refreshed with more boiling water and yeast extract.)
2. Mince the spring onion (scallion) and garlic. Cut the green pepper into thin strips. Slice the mushrooms.
3. When the tofu has defrosted, squeeze it gently and slice it. Retain the soaking liquid.
4. Heat 1 tablespoon oil in a saucepan and add the tofu. Fry the slices for a minute, then turn over and fry the other side for a minute. Add the spring onion (scallion), garlic, green pepper and mushrooms. Pour in 2½-3 fl oz (75-90ml)/½ cup of the yeast extract liquid. Bring to the boil, then lower heat, cover pan and simmer for about 10 minutes.
5. Slice the cooked potatoes. Heat the remaining tablespoon oil in a frying pan and sauté the potatoes until lightly browned on both sides. Season to taste.
6. Mix the cornflour (cornstarch) and water in a cup and stir it into the tofu mixture. Simmer for a minute or two until it has thickened, then dish up with the potatoes.

SATURDAY LUNCH

Mediterranean-style Courgette (Zucchini) Salad

Imperial (Metric)

½ lb (225g) courgettes
1 tablespoon olive oil
1 teaspoon lemon juice
¼ teaspoon garlic salt
Freshly ground black pepper
1 teaspoon dried or 1 tablespoon
  minced fresh mint

American

½ pound zucchini
1 tablespoon olive oil
1 teaspoon lemon juice
¼ teaspoon garlic salt
Freshly ground black pepper
1 teaspoon dried or 1 tablespoon
  minced fresh mint

1. Halve the courgettes (zucchini) across their width, then slice into thick matchsticks. Cook them in just enough water to cover the bottom of the pan for 2-3 minutes and drain.
2. In a bowl combine the oil, lemon juice, garlic salt, pepper to taste and mint. Add the courgettes (zucchini) while still warm and mix well. Chill thoroughly. (Nice with thick slabs of wholemeal/whole wheat bread.)

Week 4

SHOPPING LIST

Vegetables and Fruit

½ lb (225g) new potatoes
Spring onions (scallions)
2 small courgettes (zucchini)
5 small onions
1 small tomato
¼ lb (115g) rhubarb
½ lb (225g)/½ cup green beans
Garlic
Lemon
Celery
1 small leek
Parsley
¼ lb (115g)/2 cups mushrooms
2 oz (55g)/⅓ cup broad (fava) beans
  (about 6 oz (170g)/1 cup before
  shelling)
Salad ingredients

Miscellaneous

15½ oz (440g) tin (can)
  haricot (navy) beans
Vegan mayonnaise
Soya (soy) yogurt
9-10 oz (255-285g) tofu
Dates
Creamed coconut
1 oz (30g) roasted cashews
Bulgur wheat
1 oz (30g) pine (pignolia) nuts

Check that you have all the staples listed on page 13

SUNDAY LUNCH

Bean and Potato Salad

Imperial (Metric)	American
½ lb (225g) new potatoes	½ pound new potatoes
1-2 spring onions	1-2 scallions
½ x 15½ oz (440g) tin haricot beans	½ x 15½ ounce can navy beans
1 tablespoon vegan mayonnaise	1 tablespoon vegan mayonnaise
⅛ pint (70ml) soya yogurt	⅓ cup soy yogurt
Black pepper to taste	Black pepper to taste

1. Scrub the potatoes and cook them in lightly salted water until tender. Drain them and when cool enough to handle dice them.
2. Chop the spring onions (scallions) finely. Put them in a bowl with the potatoes. Add the beans (drained), mayonnaise, yogurt and seasoning. Mix well, then chill thoroughly. (As an accompaniment, crispbread provides a particularly nice contrast in texture.)

SUNDAY DINNER

Courgette (Zucchini) and Tomato Flan

Imperial (Metric)

1½ oz (45g) wholemeal flour*
¾ oz (15g) vegan margarine*
Pinch sea salt
1 small onion
1 tablespoon vegetable oil
1 small courgette
3 oz (85g) tofu
1 tablespoon autolized yeast
   flakes or powder
½ teaspoon basil
Sea salt and freshly ground black
   pepper to taste
1 small tomato

American

⅓ cup whole wheat flour*
1/6 cup vegan margarine*
Pinch sea salt
1 small onion
1 tablespoon vegetable oil
1 small zucchini
⅓ cup tofu
1 tablespoon Good-Tasting Yeast
½ teaspoon sweet basil
Sea salt and freshly ground black
   pepper to taste
1 small tomato

1. Combine the flour, margarine and salt and add enough water to make pastry. Roll out and place in a small greased flan tin.
2. Chop the onion and sauté it for about 5 minutes in the oil. Slice the courgette (zucchini) and add it to the pan, continue to cook for 3-4 minutes longer.
3. Prick the pastry with a fork and bake it for about 5 minutes at 400°F (200° C)/Gas Mark 6.
4. Mash the tofu. Mix with the yeast, basil and seasoning, then stir into the vegetables.
5. Skin and slice the tomato. Stir it into the mixture. Turn this into the flan case. Lower oven heat to 375°F (190°C)/Gas Mark 5 and bake for about half an hour. Accompany the flan with a side salad.

*If making the whole week's menus then use 4 oz (115g)/1 cup flour and 2 oz (55g)/¼ cup margarine to make the pastry. Use just over one third of it for this recipe; wrap the remainder in clingfilm and refrigerate.

SUNDAY DESSERT

Rhubarb and Date Cream

Imperial (Metric)	*American*
4 oz (115g) rhubarb	¼ pound rhubarb
2 oz (55g) dates	⅓ cup dates
4 tablespoons water	4 tablespoons water
1 oz (30g) creamed coconut	1 ounce creamed coconut

1. Chop the rhubarb and dates. Cook them with the water at low heat for 10-15 minutes.
2. Grate or chop the creamed coconut and add it to the saucepan. Beat well. Spoon the mixture into a dessert bowl; cool, then chill.

MONDAY

Cashew and Vegetable Curry

Imperial (Metric)	American
2½-3 oz (65-85g) brown rice*	½ cup brown rice*
1 small carrot	1 small carrot
1 small courgette	1 small zucchini
2 oz (55g) green beans	2 ounces green beans
4 tablespoons water	4 tablespoons water
1 small onion	1 small onion
1 small clove garlic	1 small clove garlic
1 tablespoon vegetable oil	1 tablespoon vegetable oil
½ teaspoon ground coriander	½ teaspoon ground coriander
½ teaspoon ground cumin	½ teaspoon ground cumin
½ teaspoon turmeric	½ teaspoon turmeric
¼ teaspoon powdered ginger	¼ teaspoon powdered ginger
⅛ teaspoon chilli powder	⅛ teaspoon chili powder
1 tablespoon tomato purée	1 tablespoon tomato paste
1 teaspoon lemon juice	1 teaspoon lemon juice
2 tablespoons soya yogurt	2 tablespoons soy yogurt
1 oz (30g) roasted cashew nuts**	¼ cup roasted cashew nuts**

1. Cook the rice until tender.
2. Chop the carrot, courgette (zucchini) and beans and cook them in the water until just tender.
3. Chop the onion; mince the garlic. Sauté them in the oil in a saucepan for 3-4 minutes. Stir in all the spices and cook over a very low heat for another minute. Stir in the tomato purée (paste) and lemon juice.
4. Add the vegetables to the pan, along with their cooking liquid. Cook, uncovered, for another minute or two.
5. Stir in the yogurt and heat gently without boiling. Add the cashews and pour over the cooked rice. (This is nice with chutney.)

*If making the whole week's menus then cook double this quantity, cool and then refrigerate half of it for use on Friday.

**If buying the salted kind then it's a good idea to wash the salt off before using. Raw ones can be roasted under the grill (broiler).

TUESDAY

Tofu and Vegetable Stew

Imperial (Metric)	American
2 oz (55g) green beans*	2 ounces green beans*
1 small carrot*	1 small carrot*
1 stick celery*	1 stalk celery*
1 small onion*	1 small onion*
1 tablespoon vegetable oil*	1 tablespoon vegetable oil*
3-4 oz (85-115g) tofu*	⅓-½ cup tofu*
1 tablespoon wholemeal flour*	1 tablespoon whole wheat flour*
1 tablespoon soya sauce*	1 tablespoon soy sauce*
½ teaspoon sage*	½ teaspoon sage*
Sea salt and freshly ground black pepper to taste	Sea salt and freshly ground black pepper to taste
Wholemeal bread, rice or bulgur wheat to serve (optional)	Whole wheat bread, rice or bulgur wheat to serve (optional)

1. Chop the beans, carrot and celery. Cover with boiling water and cook until crisp-tender. Drain, retaining the stock.
2. Chop the onion. Sauté in the oil for about 3 minutes. Dice the tofu and add it to the pan. Sauté for a few minutes longer, stirring frequently. Sprinkle in the flour and stir. Gradually add ⅛ pint (70ml)/⅔ cup vegetable stock*. Stir until thickened.
3. Add the soya (soy) sauce, sage, seasoning and the cooked vegetables to the pan. Stir well and simmer, uncovered, for 3-4 minutes longer. Accompany with wedges of bread or serve over cooked rice or bulgur wheat.

If making the whole week's dishes then double all of these ingredients and refrigerate half the stew for use on Thursday.

WEDNESDAY

Bulgur, Bean and Celery Casserole

Imperial (Metric)	American
2½ oz (70g) bulgur wheat	½ cup bulgur wheat
1 small onion	1 small onion
1 tablespoon vegetable oil	1 tablespoon vegetable oil
1 small clove garlic	1 small clove garlic
2 oz (55g) mushrooms	1 cup mushrooms
2 sticks celery	2 stalks celery
1 teaspoon rosemary	1 teaspoon rosemary
½ × 15½ oz (440g) tin haricot beans	½ × 15½ ounce can navy beans
1 teaspoon lemon juice	1 teaspoon lemon juice
Freshly ground black pepper	Freshly ground black pepper

1. Cook the bulgur wheat in about three times its volume of water (the exact amount never seems to make much difference) and a little sea salt. (This should only take a few minutes.)
2. Chop the onion. Sauté it in the oil in a largish saucepan for 2-3 minutes. Crush the garlic and add it to the pan; cook for a minute or two longer.
3. Slice the mushrooms. Chop the celery. Add them to the pan along with the rosemary (N.B. dried rosemary is best ground with a pestle and mortar before use). Stir well, cover pan, lower heat and leave to cook for a few minutes.
4. Drain and rinse the beans. Add them to the pan along with the lemon juice and pepper to taste. Stir well and heat for a couple of minutes, then stir in the cooked bulgur wheat. Mix and cook for a couple of minutes more; taste for seasoning before dishing up.

THURSDAY

Tofu Pot Pie

Imperial (Metric)	American
Pastry made from 2½ oz (70g) wholemeal flour and 1¼ oz (35g) vegan margarine or the remaining pastry from Sunday's flan (page 48)	Pastry made from ½ cup whole wheat flour and ¼ cup vegan margarine or the remaining pastry from Sunday's flan (page 48)
Tofu stew (see Tuesday, page 51)	Tofu stew (see Tuesday, page 51)

1. Roll out about two-thirds of the pastry on a floured board and put it into a small, oiled deep pie dish. Prick the pastry and bake it at 450°F (230° C)/Gas Mark 8 for about 5 minutes.
2. Meanwhile, roll out the rest of the pastry. Remove the pie dish from the oven and reduce oven heat to 400°F (200°C)/Gas Mark 6. Spoon the tofu stew mixture into the pastry and top with the remainder of the pastry. Prick with a fork and bake for about 25 minutes.

FRIDAY

Mediterranean-style Fried Rice

Imperial (Metric)	American
1 oz (30g) pine nuts*	2 tablespoons pignolia nuts*
1 small onion	1 small onion
1 small leek	1 small leek
1 tablespoon olive oil	1 tablespoon olive oil
2½-3 oz (70-85g) brown rice, cooked	½ cup brown rice, cooked
Juice and grated rind of ½ small lemon	Juice and grated rind of ½ small lemon
2 teaspoons tomato purée	2 teaspoons tomato paste
Sea salt and freshly ground black pepper to taste	Sea salt and freshly ground black pepper to taste
2 teaspoons minced parsley	2 teaspoons minced parsley

1. Toast the nuts lightly under the grill (broiler). Set aside.
2. Chop the onion and cleaned leek. Sauté them in the oil for 2-3 minutes.
3. Add the rice, lemon juice and rind, tomato purée (paste) and seasoning. Stir well. Cook the mixture over a fairly low heat for 7-10 minutes, stirring frequently.
4. Stir in the parsley and toasted nuts and dish up immediately.

*These are undeniably very expensive, but they are so rich that a small amount of them goes a long way, and their flavour is unique.

SATURDAY LUNCH

Bean and Mushroom Salad

Imperial (Metric)	American
2 oz (55g) green beans	2 ounces green beans
2 oz (55g) broad beans (about 6 oz (170g) before shelling)	2 ounces fava beans (about 6 ounces before shelling)
2 oz (55g) button mushrooms	2 ounces button mushrooms
1½ tablespoons vegan mayonnaise	1½ tablespoons vegan mayonnaise
1 tablespoon soya yogurt	1 tablespoon soy yogurt
Sea salt and freshly ground black pepper to taste	Sea salt and freshly ground black pepper to taste

1. Top and tail the green beans and slice them into bite-sized pieces. Cook until crisp-tender and drain.
2. Cook the shelled broad (fava) beans until tender and drain.
3. Clean and slice the mushrooms.
4. Put all of the beans and the mushrooms into a bowl; add the mayonnaise and yogurt, stir well and season to taste. Chill.

Week 5

SHOPPING LIST

Vegetables and Fruit

Spring onions (scallions)
Parsley
Mixed salad ingredients
6 small onions
6-8 oz (170-225g) seasonal green
    vegetable
6 oz (170g) plums
2 small courgettes (zucchini)
4 small tomatoes
Garlic
¼ cucumber*
1 small carrot
2 oz (55g)/1 cup mushrooms

Miscellaneous

4 oz (115g)/¾ cup mixed nuts
9-10 oz (255-285g) tofu
Peanut butter
1 × 15½ oz (440g) tin (can) chick
    peas (garbanzo beans)
Mango chutney
Smokey Snaps (imitation bacon bits)
3 oz (85g)/½ cup red lentils
7 oz (200g) tin (can) tomatoes
Soya (soy) yogurt

Check that you have all the staples listed on page 13

*⅛ for recipe; use the rest as part of the mixed salad ingredients

SUNDAY LUNCH

Nut Balls and Salad

Imperial (Metric)

2 oz (55g) mixed nuts
1 oz (30g) wholemeal breadcrumbs
1 teaspoon olive oil
2 teaspoons tomato purée
1 spring onion
1 tablespoon parsley
Mixed salad ingredients

American

½ cup mixed nuts
½ cup fresh whole wheat
  breadcrumbs
1 teaspoon olive oil
2 teaspoons tomato paste
1 scallion
1 tablespoon parsley
Mixed salad ingredients

1. Grind the nuts. In a bowl mix the nuts and breadcrumbs, and add the oil and tomato purée (paste).
2. Mince the spring onion (scallion) and parsley and add them to the bowl. Mix well, then knead with the hands, and form into walnut-sized balls. Refrigerate, then serve on top of a mixed salad.

SUNDAY DINNER

Scalloped Tofu au Gratin

Imperial (Metric)	American
¾ oz (20g) hard vegan margarine (e.g., Tomor)*	1½ tablespoons hard vegan margarine*
1 oz (30g) soya flour*	¼ cup soy flour*
½-¾ teaspoon yeast extract*	½-¾ teaspoon yeast extract*
1 small onion	1 small onion
2 tablespoons vegetable oil	2 tablespoons vegetable oil
5-6 oz (140-170g) firm tofu	¾ cup firm tofu
1 tablespoon wholemeal flour	1 tablespoon whole wheat flour
4 fl oz (115ml) soya milk	½ cup soymilk
Sea salt and freshly ground black pepper to taste	Sea salt and freshly ground black pepper to taste
1½ oz (45g) wholemeal breadcrumbs	¾ cup fresh whole wheat breadcrumbs
1 tablespoon autolized yeast flakes	1 tablespoon Good Tasting Yeast flakes or powder
6-8 oz (170-225g) seasonal green vegetable	6-8 ounces seasonal green vegetable

1. Melt the margarine in a small saucepan over a low heat. Remove from heat and stir in the soya (soy) flour and yeast extract. Pour the mixture onto an oiled flat tin or plate; cool then chill until ready to use.
2. Chop the onion finely and sauté it in half the oil in a frying pan (skillet) for 2-3 minutes. Dice the tofu and add it to the frying pan (skillet). Sauté for a further 2-3 minutes, stirring frequently. Remove from heat.
3. In a small saucepan heat the remaining tablespoon of oil and stir in the flour. Gradually add the milk, stirring constantly to avoid lumps. When boiling and thickened add seasoning. Remove from heat.
4. Dice the soya flour mixture finely. Add half to the white sauce and stir well. Season to taste, then stir in the tofu and onion.
5. Turn the mixture into an oiled baking dish. Mix the breadcrumbs with the dry yeast and sprinkle on top along with the remainder of the diced soya (soy) flour mixture.
6. Bake at 350°F (180°C)/Gas Mark 4 for 20-30 minutes, until lightly browned on top. Accompany with a lightly-steamed seasonal green vegetable.

*If making the whole week's menus then double these ingredients; follow the instructions under 1 above; when chilled cut in half and keep half of it in the refrigerator until required.

SUNDAY DESSERT

Nutty Plum Crumble

Imperial (Metric)	American
1 oz (30g) wholemeal flour	¼ cup whole wheat flour
¼ oz (20g) rolled oats	1/6 cup rolled oats
Raw cane sugar to taste	Raw cane sugar to taste
½ oz (15g) vegan margarine	1 tablespoon vegan margarine
½ oz (15g) peanut butter	1 tablespoon peanut butter
6 oz (170g) plums	6 ounces plums
1 tablespoon water	1 tablespoon water

1. Put the flour, oats and sugar in a bowl. Rub in the margarine and peanut butter finely.
2. Slice the plums. Put them in a baking dish with the water. Cover with the crumble mixture. Bake at 375°F (180°C)/Gas Mark 5 for about half an hour until lightly browned on top.

Greek-style Courgette (Zucchini) and Chick Pea (Garbanzo Bean) Stew

Imperial (Metric)	American
2½-3 oz (70-85g) brown rice*	½ cup brown rice*
1 small onion	1 small onion
1 tablespoon olive oil	1 tablespoon olive oil
1 small courgette	1 small zucchini
2 small tomatoes	2 small tomatoes
2 teaspoons tomato purée	2 teaspoons tomato paste
½ teaspoon marjoram	½ teaspoon marjoram
Sea salt and freshly ground black pepper to taste	Sea salt and freshly ground black pepper to taste
½ × 15½ oz (440g) tin chick peas	½ × 15½ ounce can garbanzo beans
⅛ pint (70ml) water	⅓ cup water

1. Cook the rice until tender.
2. Slice the onion thinly. Sauté it in the oil in a saucepan for 2-3 minutes. Slice the courgette (zucchini) thinly and add it to the pan. Sauté for a further 4-5 minutes.
3. Skin and chop the tomatoes. Add them to the saucepan with the purée (paste), marjoram, and the seasoning. Then add the chick peas (beans) and water, and stir well. Bring to the boil, then lower heat and simmer, uncovered, for about 15 minutes.
4. Serve the stew over the rice.

*If making the whole week's menus then cook double this quantity of rice, cool and refrigerate half.

TUESDAY

Rich Nut Rissoles

Imperial (Metric)	American
¾ oz (20g) hard vegan margarine (e.g. Tomor)*	1½ tablespoons hard vegan margarine*
1 oz (30g) soya flour*	¼ cup soy flour*
½-¾ teaspoon yeast extract*	½-¾ teaspoon yeast extract*
2 oz (55g) mixed nuts	½ cup mixed nuts
1 small onion	1 small onion
1 tablespoon vegetable oil (plus additional for frying rissoles)	1 tablespoon vegetable oil (plus additional for frying rissoles)
1 tablespoon wholemeal flour	1 tablespoon whole wheat flour
2 tablespoons soya milk	2 tablespoons soymilk
1 oz (30g) wholemeal breadcrumbs	½ cup fresh whole wheat breadcrumbs
½ teaspoon marjoram	½ teaspoon marjoram
Mixed salad ingredients	Mixed salad ingredients

1. Melt the margarine in a small saucepan over a low heat. Remove from heat and stir in the soya (soy) flour and yeast extract. Pour the mixture onto an oiled flat tin or plate; cool, then chill until ready to use.
2. Grind the nuts.
3. Chop the onion finely. Sauté in the oil for 3-4 minutes. Stir in the flour and mix well, then add the milk and stir until thickened. Chop the soya (soy) flour mixture and stir it in as well.
4. Remove the pan from the heat and stir in the nuts, breadcrumbs and marjoram. Leave to cool while preparing the salad.
5. Form the mixture into three rissoles and shallow-fry in a little oil, turning once, so that both sides are browned. Serve with salad.

*If you made this on Sunday then simply use the refrigerated half of the mixture, skipping instruction 1 above.

WEDNESDAY

Mexican Chick Peas (Garbanzo Beans) and Bulgur Wheat

Imperial (Metric)	American
1 small onion	1 small onion
1 small clove garlic	1 small clove garlic
1 tablespoon olive oil	1 tablespoon olive oil
½ teaspoon ground cumin	½ teaspoon ground cumin
½ teaspoon oregano	½ teaspoon oregano
½ teaspoon paprika	½ teaspoon paprika
⅛-¼ teaspoon chilli powder	⅛-¼ teaspoon chili powder
2 small tomatoes	2 small tomatoes
1 tablespoon tomato purée	1 tablespoon tomato paste
½ × 15½ oz (440g) tin chick peas	½ × 15½ ounce can garbanzo beans
3-5 tablespoons water	3-5 tablespoons water
2-2½ oz (55-70g) bulgur wheat	⅓ cup bulgur wheat

1. Chop the onion and mince the garlic. Sauté them in the oil for a few minutes. Add the cumin, oregano, paprika and chilli (chili) powder and stir over very low heat for a minute.
2. Skin and chop the tomatoes. Add them to the saucepan along with the purée (paste), drained and rinsed chick peas (beans), and water. Bring to the boil, then lower heat and simmer, uncovered, for 5-10 minutes, stirring occasionally.
3. Cover the bulgur wheat with about three times its quantity in water and a pinch of sea salt, bring to the boil, lower heat, cover pan and simmer until all the water is absorbed (only a few minutes).
4. Serve the chick peas (beans) over the cooked bulgur wheat.

THURSDAY

Nasi Goreng

Imperial (Metric)	American
2½-3 oz (70-85g) brown rice	½ cup brown rice
3-4 oz (85-115g) tofu	⅓-½ cup tofu
1 tablespoon vegan margarine	1 tablespoon vegan margarine
⅛ cucumber	⅛ cucumber
1 small onion	1 small onion
1 small clove garlic	1 small clove garlic
1 tablespoon vegetable oil	1 tablespoon vegetable oil
1 teaspoon ground coriander	1 teaspoon ground coriander
1 teaspoon ground cumin	1 teaspoon ground cumin
1 tablespoon mango chutney	1 tablespoon mango chutney
2 tablespoons Smokey Snaps	2 tablespoons imitation bacon bits

1. Cook the rice (or use rice which was cooked earlier in the week).
2. Slice the tofu into thin strips. Shallow-fry in the margarine in a frying pan (skillet) until lightly browned. Set aside (keep warm if convenient). Chop the cucumber finely. Set aside.
3. Chop the onion and garlic finely. Sauté in the oil in a wok or frying pan (skillet) until beginning to turn brown. Lower heat, stir in the spices and then the rice and stir well. Cook until the rice is heated through, then stir in the chutney and Smokey Snaps (imitation bacon bits).
4. Transfer to a plate and top with the tofu strips and cucumber.

FRIDAY

Lentil and Vegetable Pottage

Imperial (Metric)	American
1 small onion	1 small onion
1 small clove garlic	1 small clove garlic
1 tablespoon vegetable oil	1 tablespoon vegetable oil
3 oz (85g) red lentils	½ cup red lentils
½ pint (285ml) water	1⅓ cups water
1 bay leaf	1 bay leaf
Sea salt and freshly ground black pepper to taste	Sea salt and freshly ground black pepper to taste
1 small courgette	1 small zucchini
1 small carrot	1 small carrot
2 oz (55g) mushrooms	1 cup mushrooms
Wholemeal bread as required	Whole wheat bread as required

1. Chop the onion. Mince the garlic. Sauté them in the oil in a saucepan for 2-3 minutes.
2. Add the lentils, water, bay leaf and seasoning. Bring to the boil, then lower heat, cover pan, and simmer for about 10 minutes.
3. Chop the courgette (zucchini), carrot and mushrooms quite finely. Add them to the saucepan, raise heat until it is fully boiling again, then lower heat, cover pan, and simmer for a further 10 minutes.
4. Serve in a large bowl (a pottage is more substantial than a lunch-time soup but is eaten with a spoon) accompanied by the bread.

SATURDAY LUNCH

Chilled Cream of Tomato Soup

Imperial (Metric)

1 small clove garlic
1 tablespoon vegan margarine
7 oz (200g) tin tomatoes
4 fl oz (115ml) soya yogurt
Freshly ground black pepper

American

1 small clove garlic
1 tablespoon vegan margarine
7 ounce can tomatoes
½ cup soy yogurt
Freshly ground black pepper

1. Chop the garlic finely. Sauté in the margarine until lightly browned.
2. Put all the ingredients in the liquidizer and blend thoroughly. Chill before serving.

Autumn/Winter Recipes

Week 1

SHOPPING LIST

Vegetables and Fruit

1 small cauliflower
1 small potato
Parsley
4 small onions
1 small courgette (zucchini)
2 small carrots
1 small banana
1 lemon
10-12 oz (285-350g) tomatoes
Black olives
Garlic
Small chunk swede (rutabaga)
2 oz (55g) mushrooms
6-8 Brussels sprouts
Fresh ginger (root)
Frozen peas
Salad ingredients

Miscellaneous

6 oz (170g) aduki beans
Sesame seeds
Broken cashews
Soya (soy) yogurt (optional)
Tabasco sauce
2 oz (55g) roasted peanuts
Gram (garbanzo bean) flour
Tahini

Check that you have all the staples listed on page 13

SUNDAY LUNCH

Cream of Cauliflower Soup

Imperial (Metric)	American
¼-⅓ small cauliflower*	¼-⅓ small cauliflower*
1 small potato	1 small potato
¼ pint (150ml) water	⅔ cup water
¼ pint (150ml) soya milk	⅔ cup soymilk
½ tablespoon vegan margarine	½ tablespoon vegan margarine
Sea salt, freshly ground black pepper and a little freshly grated nutmeg	Sea salt, freshly ground black pepper and a little freshly grated nutmeg
1 tablespoon chopped parsley	1 tablespoon chopped parsley

1. Chop the cauliflower and potato (peeled if preferred, but it's not really necessary).
2. Put the vegetables into a saucepan with the water; bring to the boil, lower heat, cover pan, and simmer for about 15 minutes, until the potato is soft.
3. Empty the contents of the saucepan into a liquidizer, add the soya (soy) milk, and blend thoroughly.
4. Return to the saucepan and re-heat gently. Stir in the margarine and seasoning.
5. Serve immediately, sprinkled with parsley.

*The rest will be used later in the week (see pages 73 and 74).

SUNDAY DINNER

Aduki Bean and Vegetable Crumble

Imperial (Metric)	American
2 oz (55g) aduki beans*	¼ cup aduki beans*
1 small onion	1 small onion
1 tablespoon oil	1 tablespoon oil
1 small carrot	1 small carrot
1 small courgette	1 small zucchini
¼ teaspoon sage	¼ teaspoon sage
2 teaspoons soya sauce	2 teaspoons soy sauce
1 oz (30g) vegan margarine	⅛ cup vegan margarine
2 oz (55g) wholemeal flour	½ cup whole wheat flour
1 tablespoon sesame seeds	1 tablespoon sesame seeds
Sea salt and freshly ground	Sea salt and freshly ground
black pepper to taste	black pepper to taste

1. In the morning cover the beans with boiling water and leave to soak for several hours. Then drain the water, cover with lots of fresh cold water, bring to the boil, lower heat and simmer for about 45 minutes until soft. Add a little sea salt only at the end of the cooking time.
2. Chop the onion and sauté it briefly in the oil in a saucepan. Dice the carrot and courgette (zucchini) and add them to the saucepan. Sauté for about 3-4 minutes.
3. Add the sage, soya (soy) sauce and drained beans to the saucepan and stir well. Remove from heat and set aside.
4. Rub the margarine into the flour finely. Stir in the sesame seeds and seasoning to taste.
5. Put the bean mixture into a greased casserole or baking dish and cover with the crumble mixture. Bake at 400°F (200°C)/Gas Mark 6 for about half an hour.

*If preparing the whole week's menus then soak and cook 6 oz (175g)/¾ cup beans; use a third of them for this dish and store the remainder (in the liquid they were cooked in) in the fridge until required.

SUNDAY DESSERT

Baked Banana Halves

Imperial (Metric)	*American*
1 teaspoon vegan margarine	1 teaspoon vegan margarine
1 small banana	1 small banana
1 teaspoon lemon juice	1 teaspoon lemon juice
1 tablespoon raw sugar	1 tablespoon raw sugar
Pinch ground cinnamon	Pinch ground cinnamon
Handful cashew pieces	Handful cashew pieces
Soya yogurt (optional)	Soy yogurt (optional)

1. Heat the margarine in a baking dish in a 400°F (200°C)/Gas Mark 6 oven for about 5 minutes.
2. Slice the banana in half lengthwise and turn the halves in the margarine so they are well coated.
3. Sprinkle the banana halves with lemon juice, sugar, cinnamon and cashew pieces. Bake in the oven for about 15 minutes.
4. Serve immediately, topped with soya (soy) yogurt if desired.

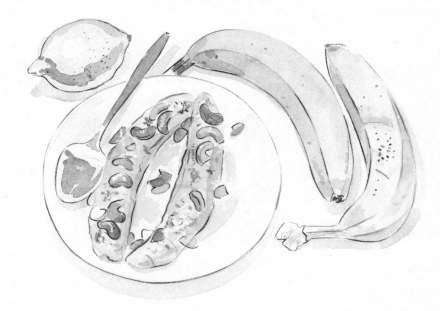

MONDAY

Spaghetti with Olive Sauce

Imperial (Metric)	American
6 oz (170g) very ripe tomatoes	6 ounces very ripe tomatoes
4-6 black olives	4-6 black olives
1 clove garlic	1 clove garlic
2 tablespoons olive oil	2 tablespoons olive oil
¼ teaspoon oregano	¼ teaspoon oregano
Freshly ground black pepper	Freshly ground black pepper
1 tablespoon minced parsley	1 tablespoon minced parsley
3 oz (85g) wholemeal spaghetti	3 ounces whole wheat spaghetti

1. Pour boiling water over the tomatoes, leave for a minute, drain, run under cold water and skin.
2. Chop the tomatoes coarsely. Chop the olives finely. Crush the garlic.
3. Heat the oil in a saucepan. Add the tomatoes, olives, garlic, oregano and pepper. Simmer, uncovered, over a low heat for about 15 minutes, stirring occasionally. Add the parsley and cook for 2 minutes longer.
4. Meanwhile, cook the spaghetti, and when it is ready drain it and pour the sauce over it. This is nice accompanied by a side salad.

TUESDAY

Vegetable Stew

Imperial (Metric)	American
1 small onion	1 small onion
Small chunk swede	Small chunk rutabaga
1 small carrot	1 small carrot
2 oz (55g) mushrooms	1 cup mushrooms
6-8 Brussels sprouts	6-8 Brussels sprouts
1 tablespoon vegetable oil	1 tablespoon vegetable oil
Few sprigs cauliflower	Few sprigs cauliflower
1 tablespoon tomato purée	1 tablespoon tomato paste
½ teaspoon marjoram	½ teaspoon marjoram
1 bay leaf	1 bay leaf
Freshly ground black pepper	Freshly ground black pepper
¼ pint (150ml) water	⅔ cup water
Soya sauce to taste	Soy sauce to taste
Wholemeal bread as required	Whole wheat bread as required

1. Chop the onion finely. Dice the swede (rutabaga) and carrot into roughly the same size. Slice the mushrooms. Halve the sprouts.
2. Heat the oil in a saucepan and add the vegetables. Stir well for 2-3 minutes. Add the tomato purée (paste), the herbs and the pepper, then pour in the water. Stir well, bring to the boil, lower heat, cover pan, and simmer for 15-20 minutes, by which time most or all of the water should have been absorbed and the vegetables all be tender.
3. Stir in a little soya (soy) sauce to taste, and serve immediately, accompanied by thick slices of bread.

WEDNESDAY

Cauliflower and Pea Curry

Imperial (Metric)	American
Remainder of cauliflower — 4-6 oz (100-150g)	Remainder of cauliflower — 4-6 ounces
1 small onion	1 small onion
1 tablespoon vegan margarine	1 tablespoon vegan margarine
1 clove garlic	1 clove garlic
¼-inch piece fresh ginger	¼-inch piece ginger root
½ teaspoon ground coriander	½ teaspoon ground coriander
½ teaspoon ground cumin	½ teaspoon ground cumin
¼ teaspoon garam masala	¼ teaspoon garam masala
¼ teaspoon chilli powder (or more to taste)	¼ teaspoon chili powder (or more to taste)
1 tablespoon tomato purée	1 tablespoon tomato paste
4 tablespoons water	4 tablespoons water
Sea salt to taste	Sea salt to taste
2 oz (55g) frozen peas	⅓ cup frozen peas
1 tablespoon soya milk	1 tablespoon soymilk
2½-3 oz (70-85g) brown rice*	⅓-½ cup brown rice*

1. Chop the cauliflower into florets and cook in a very little water for about 5 minutes. Drain.
2. Grate the onion coarsely. Heat the margarine in a saucepan and add the onion. Cook briefly until beginning to change colour. Meanwhile, crush the garlic and grate or finely chop the ginger. Add them to the saucepan and stir well. Cook for another minute or so.
3. Stir in the spices and cook for about 30 seconds longer. Then add the tomato purée (paste) and water, plus a little salt if required. Bring to the boil, then stir in the cauliflower and peas. Lower heat, cover pan, and cook for about 5 minutes, until the cauliflower and peas are tender. Stir in the soya (soy) milk and serve over rice, accompanied by mango chutney and a papadum if desired.

*If preparing the week's menus then cook a double amount of rice and store half of it (after cooling) in the fridge.

THURSDAY

Aduki Beans, Rice and Tomatoes

Imperial (Metric)	American
1 small onion	1 small onion
1 clove garlic	1 clove garlic
1 tablespoon oil	1 tablespoon oil
4-6 oz (150-170g) tomatoes	4-6 ounces tomatoes
2 oz (55g) aduki beans, cooked	¼ cup aduki beans, cooked
2½-3 oz (70-85g) brown rice, cooked	⅓-½ cup brown rice, cooked
2 teaspoons soya sauce	2 teaspoons soy sauce
½ teaspoon cider vinegar	½ teaspoon cider vinegar
Black pepper to taste	Black pepper to taste
Few drops Tabasco sauce	Few drops Tabasco sauce

1. Chop the onion and garlic. Sauté in the oil in a saucepan until beginning to brown.
2. Skin and chop the tomatoes. Add them to the pan and cook for 2-3 minutes longer.
3. Add the drained beans and cooked rice to the pan and cook for a few minutes longer. Add the soya (soy) sauce, vinegar, pepper and Tabasco sauce and stir well before serving.

FRIDAY

Peanut Sausages

Imperial (Metric)	American
2 oz (55g) roasted peanuts*	⅓ cup roasted peanuts*
2 oz (55g) wholemeal breadcrumbs	2 ounces whole wheat breadcrumbs
1 tablespoon gram flour	1 tablespoon garbanzo bean flour
3 teaspoons tomato purée	3 teaspoons tomato paste
¼ teaspoon marjoram	¼ teaspoon marjoram
1 teaspoon soya sauce	1 teaspoon soy sauce
4 tablespoons water	¼ cup water
Vegetable oil as required	Vegetable oil as required
Salad ingredients	Salad ingredients

1. Grind the peanuts. Put them in a bowl with the breadcrumbs, gram (garbanzo bean) flour, tomato purée (paste), marjoram and soya (soy) sauce. Add the water and stir well.
2. Form the mixture into sausage shapes. Heat a little oil in a frying pan (skillet) and fry the sausages for 5-7 minutes, turning frequently. Serve with a side salad.

*The best kind of peanuts to use are the dry-roasted unsalted ones available at some wholefood shops. Second-best (because they are so much more time-consuming) is to buy nuts in shells and shell them. If neither of those alternatives are possible then get roasted salted peanuts, rinse them as thoroughly as possible and dry them on kitchen paper.

SATURDAY LUNCH

Aduki Spread

Imperial (Metric)	*American*
2 oz (55g) aduki beans, cooked	¼ cup aduki beans, cooked
½ tablespoon oil	½ tablespoon oil
2 teaspoons soya sauce	2 teaspoons soy sauce
3 teaspoons tahini	3 teaspoons tahini
1 tablespoon minced parsley	1 tablespoon minced parsley
Wholemeal toast	Whole wheat toast

1. Drain the beans and put them in a bowl. Mash them lightly.
2. Heat the oil in a saucepan. Add the beans, soya (soy) sauce, tahini and parsley. Mix well and cook over a low heat for 5-7 minutes, stirring occasionally, by which time the mixture should have thickened.
3. Remove from heat. Serve warm on toast.

Week 2

SHOPPING LIST

Vegetables and Fruit

2 small leeks
4 small onions
6 oz (175g) mushrooms
1 cooking apple
3 small carrots
3 oz (85g) broccoli
9-10 oz (255-285g)/9-10 ounces
   potatoes
1 green pepper
4 oz (115g) tomatoes
Garlic
Frozen peas
⅛ cucumber
Lemon
Seasonal vegetables as desired
   (for Sunday dinner)

Miscellaneous

8-12 oz (225-340g)/1-1½ cups firm
   tofu
Made mustard
2 oz (55g)/½ cup walnuts
1 oz (30g)/¼ cup sunflower seeds
Rolled oats
Maple syrup
Cashews
Semolina (farina)
7 oz (200g) tin (can) red kidney beans
Desiccated (grated) coconut
6 oz (170g)/1½ cups wholemeal
   (whole wheat) macaroni
2 oz (55g)/½ cup almonds
Roasted peanuts
Peanut butter
Tabasco sauce

Check that you have all the staples listed on page 13

SUNDAY LUNCH

Scrambled Tofu and Leek

Imperial Metric

1 small leek
3 teaspoons vegan margarine
4-6 oz (115-170g) firm tofu*
1 teaspoon turmeric
2 teaspoons soya sauce
2 teaspoons made mustard
Freshly ground black pepper
Wholemeal toast as required

American

1 small leek
3 teaspoons vegan margarine
½-¾ cup firm tofu*
1 teaspoon turmeric
2 teaspoons soy sauce
2 teaspoons made mustard
Freshly ground black pepper
Whole wheat toast as required

1. Wash and chop the leek finely. Heat the margarine in a saucepan and add the leek. Stir well, then cover pan, and cook over a very low heat for about five minutes.
2. Mash the tofu in a small bowl with the turmeric, soya (soy) sauce, mustard and pepper to taste.
3. Add the tofu mixture to the saucepan and mix well. Cook until the tofu mixture is well heated and serve immediately over hot toast.

*If making the whole week's menus then slice the remaining 4-6 oz (115g-170g)/½-¾ cup of the tofu into 2 or 3 pieces and place in the freezer until required.

SUNDAY DINNER

Walnut and Mushroom Roast

Imperial (Metric)	American
1 small onion	1 small onion
2 oz (55g) mushrooms	1 cup mushrooms
1 tablespoon vegetable oil	1 tablespoon vegetable oil
1 oz (30g) walnuts	¼ cup walnuts
1 oz (30g) sunflower seeds	¼ cup sunflower seeds
⅛ pint (65ml) soya milk	⅓ cup soymilk
2 oz (55g) wholemeal breadcrumbs	1 cup whole wheat breadcrumbs
⅛ teaspoon sage	⅛ teaspoon sage
¼ teaspoon basil	¼ teaspoon sweet basil
Sea salt to taste	Sea salt to taste

1. Chop the onion and mushrooms finely. Sauté over low heat in the oil for about 3 minutes, until tenderized.
2. Chop the walnuts coarsely. Grind the sunflower seeds finely.
3. Add all the rest of the ingredients to the onions and mushrooms, and mix well. Transfer to a greased baking dish and bake in a 350°F (180°C)/Gas Mark 4 oven for about 45 minutes. Serve with Creamy Gravy (see recipe right) if desired and seasonal vegetables. (The water used in cooking the vegetables can be kept refrigerated for use as stock later in the week.)

Creamy Gravy

Imperial (Metric)

½ oz (15g) rolled oats
⅛ pint (65ml) warm water
1 teaspoon vegetable oil
½ teaspoon (or more to taste)
  yeast extract

American

⅛ cup rolled oats
⅓ cup warm water
1 teaspoon vegetable oil
½ teaspoon (or more to taste)
  yeast extract

1. Put the oats, water and oil in a liquidizer and blend thoroughly.
2. Pour the mixture into a small saucepan and heat gently, stirring constantly until it has thickened. Stir in the yeast extract. If the mixture is too thick add a little more water. (N.B. This can be made earlier and reheated when serving the roast.)

SUNDAY DESSERT

Baked Maple Apple Halves

Imperial (Metric)	American
1 cooking apple	1 soft tart apple
2 teaspoons water	2 teaspoons water
2 tablespoons maple syrup	2 tablespoons maple syrup
1 teaspoon vegan margarine	1 teaspoon vegan margarine

1. Halve the apple cross-wise and core it.
2. Put the water in the bottom of a greased baking dish. Put the apple halves in the dish, cut side up. Pour a tablespoon of maple syrup over each half, and dot with the margarine.
3. Bake the apple halves in a 350°F (180°C)/Gas Mark 4 oven for 40-45 minutes. If possible, baste the apple halves once or twice during this time. Serve hot.

MONDAY

Uppama (A South Indian Dish)

Imperial (Metric)	American
1 small onion	1 small onion
1 tablespoon vegetable oil	1 tablespoon vegetable oil
1 teaspoon mustard seeds	1 teaspoon mustard seeds
1 tablespoon cashew pieces	1 tablespoon broken cashews
1 teaspoon ground coriander	1 teaspoon ground coriander
½ teaspoon ground cumin	½ teaspoon ground cumin
1 teaspoon turmeric	1 teaspoon turmeric
⅛-¼ teaspoon chilli powder	⅛-¼ teaspoon chili powder
1 small carrot	1 small carrot
3 oz (85g) broccoli florets	3 ounces broccoli florets
1 teaspoon raisins	1 teaspoon raisins
½ pint (275ml) water	1⅓ cups water
Sea salt to taste	Sea salt to taste
3 oz (85g) wholemeal semolina	½ cup whole wheat farina
1-2 teaspoons vegan margarine	1-2 teaspoons vegan margarine

1. Chop the onion and sauté it in the oil in a saucepan for 2-3 minutes.
2. Add the mustard seeds and cashews and cook for a further 2 minutes.
3. Add the coriander, cumin, turmeric and chilli (chili) powder and cook for another minute.
4. Chop the carrot and broccoli quite finely. Add to the saucepan along with the raisins and stir well. Pour in the water, bring to the boil, lower heat, cover pan and cook for 3-4 minutes. Season to taste.
5. Pour in the semolina (farina) very slowly, stirring all the time. As soon as it is all in the pan and well thickened, serve it, with the margarine spread over the top so that it melts into the mixture.

TUESDAY

Irish Stew with Frozen Tofu*

Imperial (Metric)	American
4-6 oz (115-170g) frozen tofu	½-¾ cup frozen tofu
1 small onion	1 small onion
6 oz (170g) potatoes	6 ounces potatoes
1 small carrot	1 small carrot
½ teaspoon yeast extract	½ teaspoon yeast extract
¼ pint (140ml) vegetable stock or water	⅔ cup vegetable stock or water
2 oz (55g) plus 2 tablespoons wholemeal flour	½ cup plus 2 tablespoons whole wheat flour
Pinch sea salt	Pinch sea salt
1 teaspoon baking powder	1 teaspoon baking powder
½ oz (15g) vegan margarine	⅛ cup vegan margarine
Soya milk as required	Soymilk as required
1 tablespoon soya sauce	1 tablespoon soy sauce
1 tablespoon water	1 tablespoon water
1 teaspoon cider vinegar	1 teaspoon cider vinegar
1 tablespoon vegetable oil	1 tablespoon vegetable oil

1. Pour boiling water over the tofu, cover if possible, and leave for 10-15 minutes.
2. Chop the onion. Dice the potatoes and carrot into small pieces. Add the yeast extract to the stock or water and bring to the boil in a saucepan. Add the onions and potatoes, lower heat, and leave to simmer for 7-10 minutes. Add the carrots and cook for a further 4-5 minutes.
3. While the vegetables are cooking put the 2 oz (55g)/½ cup flour in a bowl and mix in salt and baking powder. Cut in the margarine, then pour in enough soya (soy) milk (about 2 tablespoons) to make a soft dough. Divide the dough into four balls.
4. Put the soya (soy) sauce, water and vinegar into a small bowl. Drain the tofu and squeeze it gently to extract excess liquid. Cut it into small dice. Put the dice into the bowl with the soya (soy) sauce mixture and stir it round; the liquid should be absorbed rapidly by the tofu.

*It must be admitted that this is rather more complicated than most of the weekday dishes featured in this book; however, it really doesn't take that long, and it is a wonderfully satisfying dish on a cold winter's night.

5. Spread the 2 tablespoons flour on a plate and turn the tofu cubes in it. Heat the oil in a frying pan (skillet) and stir-fry the tofu cubes until lightly browned.

6. Add the tofu cubes to the vegetable mixture and turn into an oven dish. Flatten the dough balls and place them on top. Place in a 425°F (220°)/Gas Mark 7 oven for 15 minutes and serve immediately.

WEDNESDAY

Jambalaya

Imperial (Metric)	American
7 oz (200g) tin red kidney beans	7 ounce can red kidney beans
½ green pepper	½ green pepper
1 tablespoon vegetable oil	1 tablespoon vegetable oil
4 oz (115g) tomatoes	¼ pound tomatoes
1 oz (30g) walnuts	¼ cup walnuts
1 oz (30g) desiccated coconut	⅓ cup grated coconut
1 teaspoon tomato purée	1 teaspoon tomato paste
1 tablespoon water	1 tablespoon water
2½-3 oz (70-85g) cooked brown rice*	¼-½ cup cooked brown rice*

1. Drain and rinse the beans.
2. Chop the pepper and sauté it in the heated oil in a saucepan for a minute or two.
3. Skin and chop the tomatoes. (The easiest way to skin tomatoes is to pour boiling water over them, and then leave them for a minute before draining them, after which the skin comes away easily — rinse them with cold water if they are too hot to handle.) Chop the walnuts coarsely.
4. Add the tomatoes, walnuts, coconut, tomato purée (paste) and water to the saucepan and stir well. Add the beans. Cover pan and leave the mixture to simmer on a very low heat for about 10 minutes, stirring occasionally. Serve over the rice.

*If making the whole week's menus then cook 5-6 oz (150-170g)/1 cup rice, and store half of it in the fridge.

THURSDAY

Macaroni and Vegetable Stew

Imperial (Metric)

3 oz (85g) wholemeal macaroni
  or other pasta shape*
1 small leek
1 small carrot
1 small potato
2 oz (55g) mushrooms
1 tablespoon vegetable oil
1 bay leaf
⅛ pint (65ml) water
½ teaspoon yeast extract

American

3 ounces whole wheat macaroni
  or other pasta shape*
1 small leek
1 small carrot
1 small potato
2 ounces mushrooms
1 tablespoon vegetable oil
1 bay leaf
⅓ cup water
½ teaspoon yeast extract

1. Cook the macaroni until tender and drain.
2. Meanwhile, dice the vegetables into small pieces. Heat the oil in a saucepan and stir-fry the vegetables for about 2 minutes. Add the bay leaf and the water, bring to the boil, lower heat, cover pan and simmer until the vegetables are tender, about 10-15 minutes.
3. Stir in the yeast extract, then add the macaroni and stir well. Cook for a couple of minutes longer, remove bay leaf and serve.

*If making the whole week's menu then cook 6 oz (170g)/1½ cups macaroni and store half of it in a container in the fridge until Saturday.

FRIDAY

Stir-fried Vegetable Rice with Almonds

Imperial (Metric)	American
2 oz (55g) almonds	½ cup almonds
1 small onion	1 small onion
1 tablespoon vegetable oil	1 tablespoon vegetable oil
1 clove garlic	1 clove garlic
½ green pepper	½ green pepper
1 small carrot	1 small carrot
2 oz (55g) mushrooms	2 ounces mushrooms
2 oz (55g) frozen peas	2 ounces frozen peas
2-3 oz (55-85g) brown rice, cooked	⅓-½ cup brown rice, cooked
3-4 teaspoons soya sauce	3-4 teaspoons soy sauce

1. Put the almonds under the grill (broiler) and toast until browned.
2. Chop the onion. Heat the oil in a frying pan (skillet) or wok and add the onion. Cook for a minute or two. Chop the garlic finely and add to the pan; sauté for 2-3 minutes longer.
3. Chop the green pepper and carrot finely. Slice the mushrooms. Add these to the pan along with the peas. Stir-fry the vegetables for 3-5 minutes.
4. Add the rice and soya (soy) sauce to the vegetables and stir well. Stir-fry for an additional 3-5 minutes.
5. Mix the almonds into the rice and serve immediately.

SATURDAY LUNCH

Macaroni Salad with an Indonesian Flavour

Imperial (Metric)	American
3-4 oz (85-115g) white cabbage	3-4 ounces white cabbage
⅛ cucumber	⅛ cucumber
3 oz (85g) wholemeal macaroni (or other pasta shape) cooked, drained and cooled	3 ounces whole wheat macaroni (or other pasta shape) cooked, drained and cooled
2-3 teaspoons roasted peanuts	2-3 teaspoons roasted peanuts
1 tablespoon peanut butter	1 tablespoon peanut butter
2 tablespoons soya milk	2 tablespoons soymilk
1 teaspoon soya sauce	1 teaspoon soy sauce
1 teaspoon lemon juice	1 teaspoon lemon juice
⅛ teaspoon garlic salt	⅛ teaspoon garlic salt
¼ teaspoon powdered ginger	¼ teaspoon powdered ginger
¼ teaspoon raw sugar	¼ teaspoon raw sugar
Few drops Tabasco sauce	Few drops Tabasco sauce

1. Grate the cabbage coarsely. Dice the cucumber finely.
2. Place the macaroni, cabbage, cucumber and peanuts in a bowl.
3. Put the remainder of the ingredients into the liquidizer and blend well.
4. Pour the peanut butter dressing over the ingredients in the bowl and mix thoroughly before serving.

Week 3

SHOPPING LIST

Vegetables and Fruit

1 aubergine (eggplant)
7 small onions
10 oz (285g)/5 cups mushrooms
Seasonal vegetables (for Sunday
    dinner)
1 pear
1 small potato (plus additional for
    Sunday and/or Thursday if desired)
1 small carrot
6 Brussels sprouts
Garlic
Fresh ginger (root)
5 small tomatoes
1 small green pepper
1 small red pepper

Miscellaneous

½ lb (225g) tempeh
1 × 7 oz (200g) tin (can) sweetcorn
Tahini
Wholemeal (whole wheat) noodles
Made mustard
Millet
Miso
1 × 15½ oz (440g) tin (can)
    chick peas (garbanzo beans)

Check that you have all the staples listed on page 13

SUNDAY LUNCH

Savoury Aubergine (Eggplant) on Toast

Imperial (Metric)

½ small aubergine
1 small onion
1 tablespoon olive oil
Sea salt and freshly ground black
  pepper to taste
Wholemeal toast

American

½ small eggplant
1 small onion
1 tablespoon olive oil
Sea salt and freshly ground black
  pepper to taste
Whole wheat toast

1. Put the halved aubergine (eggplant) cut side down on a baking dish (the remaining half should immediately be wrapped and refrigerated) and bake at 400°F (200°C)/Gas Mark 6 for about half an hour, by which time it should be soft. Leave to cool.
2. Slice the onion thinly. Fry the sliced onion in the olive oil in a frying pan (skillet) until lightly browned.
3. Scrape the aubergine (eggplant) flesh from the skin and discard the skin. Chop the flesh coarsely. Add it to the frying pan (skillet), and continue cooking for a couple of minutes longer. Season to taste and serve immediately over hot toast.

SUNDAY DINNER

Tempeh and Sweetcorn Roast with Tahini/Mushroom Sauce

Imperial (Metric)

Roast

⅛ pint (65ml) water*
1 tablespoon soya sauce*
4 oz (115g) tempeh*
1 small onion
1 tablespoon vegetable oil
½ x 7 oz (200g) tin sweetcorn
1 oz (30g) wholemeal breadcrumbs
1 tablespoon soya milk
Pinch thyme
Sea salt and freshly ground black
  pepper to taste

Sauce

2 oz (55g) mushrooms
2 teaspoons vegetable oil
2 tablespoons water
1 tablespoon tahini
2 teaspoons soya sauce

Seasonal vegetables as desired**

American

Roast

⅓ cup water*
1 tablespoon soy sauce*
½ cup tempeh*
1 small onion
1 tablespoon vegetable oil
½ cup corn kernels
½ cup fresh whole wheat
  breadcrumbs
1 tablespoon soymilk
Pinch thyme
Sea salt and freshly ground black
  pepper to taste

Sauce

1 cup mushrooms
2 teaspoons vegetable oil
2 tablespoons water
1 tablespoon tahini
2 teaspoons soy sauce

Seasonal vegetables as desired**

1. Bring the water and soya (soy) sauce to the boil in a small pan, place tempeh (defrosted if frozen) in it, lower heat, cover pan and simmer for 10 minutes; turn the tempeh over and simmer for a further 10 minutes. Drain.

*If making the whole week's menus, use double these ingredients; follow instruction 1 for the whole square of tempeh, then cool it and refrigerate until required later in the week.

**If boiling potatoes, an extra 6-8 oz (170-225g) may be cooked, cooled and refrigerated for use later in the week.

2. Chop the onion. Sauté in the oil in a saucepan 3-4 minutes until softened. Remove from heat. Mash the tempeh into the pan, then add the drained corn, breadcrumbs, milk, thyme and seasoning; mix well. Turn into an oiled oven dish and bake at 350°F (180°C)/Gas Mark 4 for about half an hour.

3. To make the sauce, chop the mushrooms and sauté them in the oil in a small pan until tender. Stir in the water, tahini, and soya (soy) sauce; bring to the boil, stirring, then lower heat and simmer for a couple of minutes. Serve the roast with the sauce poured over it, accompanied by seasonal vegetables.

SUNDAY DESSERT

Baked Pear

Imperial (Metric)

1 pear (preferably just ripe)
Raw sugar and vegan margarine as
    required
Pinch powdered ginger

American

1 pear (preferably just ripe)
Raw sugar and vegan margarine as
    required
Pinch powdered ginger

1. Peel the pear and slice it into slivers. Place in an oiled baking dish.
2. Sprinkle a little raw sugar over the top and add a few flakes of margarine and a pinch of ginger.
3. Bake at 350°F (180°C)/Gas Mark 4 for 20-30 minutes.

MONDAY

Noodles with Creamy Leek and Mushroom Sauce

Imperial (Metric)

3-3½ oz (85-100g) wholemeal noodles
1 small leek
1½ tablespoons vegan margarine
4 oz (115g) mushrooms
1½ tablespoons wholemeal flour
⅛ pint (70ml) soya milk
½ teaspoon made mustard
½ teaspoon marjoram
Sea salt and freshly ground black
  pepper to taste

American

3-3½ ounces whole wheat noodles
1 small leek
1½ tablespoons vegan margarine
2 cups mushrooms
1½ tablespoons whole wheat flour
⅓ cup soymilk
½ teaspoon made mustard
½ teaspoon marjoram
Sea salt and freshly ground black
  pepper to taste

1. Cook the noodles until tender in boiling salted water.
2. Clean and chop the leek finely. Melt 1 tablespoon margarine in a saucepan and sauté the chopped leek for 3-4 minutes.
3. Slice the mushrooms and add them to the pan; cook for a further 3-4 minutes.
4. Stir the flour into the pan, then slowly add the milk, stirring constantly (if a thinner sauce is desired add a little more than specified) until thickened and boiling. Lower heat and simmer while adding mustard, marjoram and seasoning.
5. When the noodles are cooked, drain them and toss them with the remaining ½ tablespoon margarine. Pour the sauce over them.

TUESDAY

Millet and Vegetable Stew

Imperial (Metric)	American
2½-3 oz (70-85g) millet	½ cup millet
Water as required	Water as required
Pinch sea salt	Pinch sea salt
1 small onion	1 small onion
1 tablespoon vegetable oil	1 tablespoon vegetable oil
1 small potato	1 small potato
1 small carrot	1 small carrot
6 Brussels sprouts	6 Brussels sprouts
1 teaspoon miso	1 teaspoon miso
½ teaspoon sage	½ teaspoon sage

1. Cover the millet with approximately three times its quantity in water (the exact amount really doesn't matter; you can always add a little extra at the end if necessary); add a pinch of salt. Cover, bring to the boil, then lower heat and simmer until the water is absorbed and the millet is tender (20-30 minutes).
2. Meanwhile, chop the onion and sauté it in the oil in a frying pan (skillet) or wok for 2-3 minutes. Dice the potato finely and add it to the pan; stir-fry for 3-4 minutes longer. Add two tablespoons water to the pan, cover it, and leave to simmer over a gentle heat for 5-7 minutes, checking to make sure the water doesn't dry out (add a little more if necessary).
3. Dice the carrot finely. Chop the Brussels sprouts. Add them to the pan along with another tablespoon of water. Cook — covered — for about 5 minutes longer, or until the vegetables are crisp-tender.
4. When the millet is cooked remove it from the heat and stir in the miso and sage immediately. Then add the vegetables and mix in thoroughly.

WEDNESDAY

Curried Chick Peas (Garbanzo Beans)

Imperial (Metric)	American
2½- 3 oz (70-85g) brown rice**	½ cup brown rice**
1 small onion*	1 small onion*
1 tablespoon vegetable oil*	1 tablespoon vegetable oil
1 small clove garlic*	1 small clove garlic*
¼-inch piece fresh ginger*	¼-inch piece fresh ginger root*
1 small tomato*	1 small tomato*
1 teaspoon ground cumin*	1 teaspoon ground cumin*
1 teaspoon ground coriander*	1 teaspoon ground coriander*
½ teaspoon turmeric*	½ teaspoon turmeric*
⅛-¼ teaspoon chilli powder*	⅛-¼ teaspoon chili powder*
Sea salt and freshly ground black pepper to taste*	Sea salt and freshly ground black pepper to taste*
½ × 15½ oz (440g) tin chick peas*	½ × 15½ ounce can garbanzo beans*
⅛ pint (140ml) water*	⅓ cup water*
1 bay leaf*	1 bay leaf*

1. Set the rice on to cook. Chop the onion and sauté it for 2-3 minutes in the oil in a saucepan.
2. Crush the garlic. Peel and grate the ginger finely. Chop the tomato. Add these ingredients to the pan and cook for 2-3 minutes longer. Add the spices and seasoning to the pan and stir well.
3. Drain and rinse the chick peas (garbanzo beans). Add them to the pan along with the water and bay leaf. Bring to the boil, then lower heat and simmer, uncovered, for about 10 minutes.
4. Remove the bay leaf and serve over the rice. This is nice with a papadum or chapati and mango chutney.

*If making the whole week's menus then double all of these ingredients. Follow all of the instructions above; cool and then refrigerate half the curry.

**If making the whole week's menus then cook double this amount of rice; cool and refrigerate half.

THURSDAY

Tempeh and Mushroom Stew on a Mashed Potato Base

Imperial (Metric)	American
4 oz (115g) tempeh	½ cup tempeh
1 small onion	1 small onion
1 small clove garlic	1 small clove garlic
1 tablespoon vegetable oil	1 tablespoon vegetable oil
4 oz (115g) mushrooms	2 cups mushrooms
1 small tomato	1 small tomato
1 bay leaf	1 bay leaf
1-2 teaspoons soya sauce	1-2 teaspoons soy sauce
6-8 oz (170-225g) cooked potatoes plus soya milk, vegan margarine and seasoning to taste	6-8 ounces cooked potatoes plus soy milk, vegan margarine and seasoning to taste

1. Prepare the tempeh as described in the recipe for Sunday dinner (page 92), or use tempeh previously prepared. Set aside.
2. Chop the onion and garlic and sauté in the oil for a minute or two. Slice the mushrooms, add them to the pan and cook for another minute or two.
3. Dice the tempeh. Chop the tomato. Add them to the pan, along with the bay leaf and soya (soy) sauce. Cook, uncovered, for about 5 minutes, stirring frequently.
4. Heat and mash the cooked potatoes with soya (soy) milk, margarine and seasoning to taste (or alternatively use a packet of vegan instant mashed potatoes). Make a mashed potato base, remove the bay leaf from the tempeh mixture, and pile it onto the base.

FRIDAY

Balkan Stew

Imperial (Metric)	American
1 small onion	1 small onion
1 small green pepper	1 small green pepper
1 small red pepper	1 small red pepper
1½ tablespoons vegetable oil	1½ tablespoons vegetable oil
1 small clove garlic	1 small clove garlic
2 small tomatoes	2 small tomatoes
½ small aubergine	½ small eggplant
Sea salt to taste	Sea salt to taste
Pinch cayenne pepper	Pinch cayenne pepper
3 tablespoons water	3 tablespoons water
2½-3 oz (70-85g) brown rice, cooked	½ cup brown rice, cooked

1. Slice the onion and peppers thinly. Sauté them in the oil in a saucepan for about 3 minutes.
2. Mince the garlic. Chop the tomatoes. Dice the aubergine (eggplant). Add them to the pan and cook for a couple of minutes longer.
3. Add the seasoning and then the water. Bring to the boil, then lower heat. Cover pan and simmer for about 5 minutes.
4. Stir in the cooked rice and cook, covered, for about 5 minutes longer.

SATURDAY LUNCH

Curried Chick Pea (Garbanzo Bean) and Sweetcorn Chowder

Imperial (Metric)	American
Curried chick peas from Wednesday (page 97)	Curried garbanzo beans from Wednesday (page 97)
3 tablespoons soya milk	3 tablespoons soymilk
⅛ pint (70ml) water	⅓ cup water
½ × 7 oz (200g) tin sweetcorn	About ½ cup canned corn kernels

1. Put the curried chick peas (garbanzo beans) into the liquidizer along with the milk and water. Blend thoroughly.
2. Pour into a saucepan. Add the sweetcorn (corn kernels). Heat gently, stirring occasionally until nice and hot. (This makes a very thick soup; for a thinner one add more water or soya (soy) milk.)

Week 4

SHOPPING LIST

Vegetables and Fruit

1 small carrot
9 oz (255g)/4½ cups mushrooms
Parsley
Lemon
Seasonal vegetables (for Sunday
    dinner)
5 small onions
Garlic
1 small green pepper
2 small tomatoes
1 small leek
4-6 oz (115-170g)/1-1½ cups cabbage

Miscellaneous

Bulgur wheat
Peanuts
4 oz (115g) dried chestnuts
10 oz (285g) packet tofu
Vanilla essence
Smokey Snaps
Soya (soy) yogurt
1 × 7 oz (200g) tin (can) tomatoes
1 × 15½ oz (440g) tin (can) haricot
    (navy) beans
Chinese noodles

Check that you have all the staples listed on page 13

SUNDAY LUNCH

Carroty Bulgur Salad

Imperial (Metric)	American
1½ oz (45g) bulgur wheat	¼ cup bulgur wheat
1 small carrot	1 small carrot
1 oz (30g) mushrooms	½ cup mushrooms
1 tablespoon minced parsley	1 tablespoon minced parsley
1 oz (30g) peanuts	1¾ tablespoons peanuts
1 tablespoon vegetable oil	1 tablespoon vegetable oil
1 tablespoon lemon juice	1 tablespoon lemon juice
Pinch mustard powder	Pinch mustard powder
Sea salt and freshly ground black pepper to taste	Sea salt and freshly ground black pepper to taste

1. Cover the bulgur wheat with cold water and leave to soak for an hour or longer. Drain in a tea towel (dish towel) or muslin, and squeeze well to get rid of as much moisture as possible. Transfer to a bowl.
2. Grate the carrot coarsely. Slice the mushrooms. Add both to the bulgur, along with the parsley and peanuts, and mix well.
3. In a small cup mix the oil, lemon juice and mustard powder with a fork. Pour the mixture onto the bulgur and mix thoroughly. Season to taste.

SUNDAY DINNER

Savoury Chestnut Pudding

Imperial (Metric)

2 oz (55g) dried chestnuts*
¾ oz (20g) vegan margarine
2 oz (55g) wholemeal flour
½ teaspoon baking powder
¼ pint (140ml) soya milk
Sea salt and freshly ground black
  pepper to taste
Seasonal vegetables**

American

2 ounces dried chestnuts*
1½ tablespoons vegan margarine
½ cup whole wheat flour
½ teaspoon baking powder
⅔ cup soymilk
Sea salt and freshly ground black
  pepper to taste
Seasonal vegetables**

1. Cover the chestnuts with boiling water and leave them to soak for several hours, then cook them until tender. (If the chestnuts are soaked in warm water in a wide-rimmed thermos flask, or in a warm cupboard, they may be tender enough after soaking not to require more cooking.)
2. Put the margarine in a baking dish and place in a hot oven to melt.
3. In a bowl mix the flour, baking powder, soya (soy) milk and seasoning, and add the melted margarine. Stir in the cooked drained chestnuts. Return the mixture to the baking dish and bake at 425°F (220°C)/Gas Mark 7 for 20 minutes, then lower heat to 350°F (180°C)/Gas Mark 4 and continue cooking for a further 20 minutes. Serve with seasonal vegetables to taste.

*If making the whole week's menus then use double this amount of chestnuts; follow instruction 1, then cool and refrigerate half the chestnuts in their liquid.

**If making the whole week's menus then you could buy enough cabbage to use tonight and Friday.

SUNDAY DESSERT

Sweet Tofu 'Omelette'

Imperial (Metric)

4 oz (115g) tofu
1 tablespoon soya milk
1 tablespoon wholemeal flour
¼ teaspoon baking powder
1 tablespoon raw sugar
¼ teaspoon vanilla essence
Sugar-free or raw sugar jam

American

½ cup tofu
1 tablespoon soymilk
1 tablespoon whole wheat flour
¼ teaspoon baking powder
1 tablespoon raw sugar
¼ teaspoon vanilla essence
Sugar-free or raw sugar jam

1. Put half the tofu in a liquidizer with the soya (soy) milk and blend thoroughly.
2. Put the other half of the tofu in a small mixing bowl and mash. Add the flour, baking powder, sugar, vanilla, and the blended tofu. Mix well.
3. Spread the mixture thinly in a well-greased baking dish and bake at 350°F (180°C)/Gas Mark 4 for 30-40 minutes.
4. With the help of a pancake turner carefully transfer the 'omelette' onto a serving dish. Spread jam to taste on top and eat while hot.

MONDAY

Spaghetti Ticino

Imperial (Metric)	American
3 oz (85g) wholemeal spaghetti	½ cup whole wheat spaghetti
1 small onion	1 small onion
1 small clove garlic	1 small clove garlic
1 small green pepper	1 small green pepper
1 tablespoon olive oil	1 tablespoon olive oil
2 oz (55g) mushrooms	1 cup mushrooms
1 tablespoon wholemeal flour	1 tablespoon whole wheat flour
¼ pint (140ml) soya milk	⅔ cup soymilk
Sea salt and freshly ground black pepper to taste	Sea salt and freshly ground black pepper to taste
1 teaspoon vegan margarine	1 teaspoon vegan margarine
1 tablespoon autolized yeast flakes	1 tablespoon Good Tasting yeast
2 tablespoons Smokey Snaps	2 tablespoons imitation bacon bits

1. Cook the spaghetti until just tender.
2. Meanwhile, chop the onion, garlic and green pepper finely. Sauté them in the oil in a saucepan for 3-4 minutes. Slice the mushrooms; add them to the pan and sauté the mixture for a further 2 minutes.
3. Stir in the flour, then pour in the milk slowly, stirring constantly to avoid lumps. Bring to the boil, then lower heat and simmer, uncovered, for a few minutes. Season to taste.
4. When the spaghetti is cooked, drain it and toss with the margarine and yeast.
5. Remove the sauce from the heat and stir in the Smokey Snaps (imitation bacon bits). Pour the sauce over the spaghetti.

TUESDAY

Curried Tofu

Imperial (Metric)	American
2-3 oz (55-85g) brown rice*	½ cup brown rice*
1 small onion	1 small onion
1 tablespoon vegan margarine	1 tablespoon vegan margarine
4-5 oz (115-140g) tofu	½-⅔ cup tofu
½ teaspoon ground coriander	½ teaspoon ground coriander
½ teaspoon ground cumin	½ teaspoon ground cumin
¼ teaspoon turmeric	¼ teaspoon turmeric
⅛-¼ teaspoon chilli powder	⅛-¼ teaspoon chili powder
½ teaspoon garam masala	½ teaspoon garam masala
2 tablespoons water	2 tablespoons water
1 tablespoon tomato purée	1 tablespoon tomato paste
1 tablespoon soya yogurt	1 tablespoon soy yogurt
Sea salt if required	Sea salt if required

1. Cook the rice until tender.
2. Chop the onion. Sauté it in the margarine in a saucepan for about 3 minutes. Meanwhile, drain and dice the tofu.
3. Lower heat and stir in the spices. Then add the tofu, stirring it well — but gently — so that it is well coated with the spices. After a minute or two add the water and stir in the tomato purée (paste). Cover the pan and simmer for about 10 minutes. Stir in the yogurt, taste for seasoning and add salt if needed.
4. Serve the curry over the rice (accompanied by a chapati or papadum and mango chutney if desired).

*If making the whole week's menus cook double this amount of rice; refrigerate half after it has cooled.

WEDNESDAY

Mediterranean Bean and Tomato Stew

Imperial (Metric)	American
1 small onion	1 small onion
1 small clove garlic	1 small clove garlic
1 tablespoon olive oil	1 tablespoon olive oil
7 oz (200g) tin tomatoes	7 ounce can tomatoes
1 bay leaf	1 bay leaf
1 tablespoon minced parsley	1 tablespoon minced parsley
1 teaspoon oregano	1 teaspoon oregano
½ × 15½ oz (440g) tin haricot beans	½ × 15½ ounce can navy beans
Wholemeal bread as required	Whole wheat bread as required

1. Slice the onion thinly. Crush the garlic. Sauté these ingredients in the olive oil in a saucepan for about 3 minutes.
2. Stir in the tomatoes, chopping them coarsely with the spoon while doing so. Add the bay leaf, parsley and oregano. Bring to the boil, then lower heat, cover pan and simmer for 7-10 minutes.
3. Drain the beans and add them to the pan. Cover pan again and simmer for a further 4-7 minutes. Remove bay leaf and serve accompanied by bread.

THURSDAY

Chestnut and Rice Savoury

Imperial (Metric)	*American*
1 small onion	1 small onion
1 tablespoon vegetable oil	1 tablespoon vegetable oil
1 small tomato	1 small tomato
2 oz (55g) mushrooms	1 cup mushrooms
2½-3 oz (70-85g) brown rice, cooked	½ cup brown rice, cooked
2 oz (55g) dried chestnuts, soaked and cooked (see Sunday, page 104)	2 ounces dried chestnuts, soaked and cooked (see Sunday, page 104)
2 tablespoons water	2 tablespoons water
1 teaspoon yeast extract	1 teaspoon yeast extract
1 teaspoon tomato purée	1 teaspoon tomato paste

1. Chop the onion and sauté it in the oil in a saucepan for about 3 minutes.
2. Skin and chop the tomato. Slice the mushrooms. Add them to the pan and cook for a further 3 minutes or so.
3. Add the rice and chestnuts to the pan and stir well. Then add the water, yeast extract and tomato purée (paste). Mix together very thoroughly as it heats up so that the yeast extract is amalgamated evenly into the mixture. Continue cooking over a gentle heat until all the ingredients are well heated.

FRIDAY

Chow Mein

Imperial (Metric)	American
3 oz (85g) Chinese noodles	3 ounces Chinese noodles
1 small leek	1 small leek
1 small clove garlic	1 small clove garlic
1 tablespoon vegetable oil	1 tablespoon vegetable oil
4-6 oz (115-170g) cabbage	4-6 ounces cabbage
4 oz (115g) mushrooms	2 cups mushrooms
1 tablespoon water	1 tablespoon water
1 tablespoon soya sauce	1 tablespoon soy sauce
Freshly ground black pepper	Freshly ground black pepper

1. Cook the noodles according to directions on packet; drain and rinse with cold water.
2. Chop the leek finely. Mince the garlic. Heat the oil in a wok or frying pan (skillet) and stir-fry the leek and garlic for a minute or two.
3. Shred the cabbage. Slice the mushrooms. Add these ingredients to the wok and stir-fry them for a minute or two longer. Add the water and soya (soy) sauce, lower heat, cover wok, and leave to cook for a couple of minutes.
4. Uncover the wok, raise heat, add the cooked noodles and lots of black pepper, and stir-fry for a couple of minutes longer before dishing up.

SATURDAY LUNCH

Beany Spread

Imperial (Metric)

1 small onion
1 tablespoon vegan margarine
1 small tomato
½ × 15½ oz (440g) tin haricot beans
Sea salt and freshly ground black
   pepper to taste

American

1 small onion
1 tablespoon vegan margarine
1 small tomato
½ × 15½ ounce can navy beans
Sea salt and freshly ground black
   pepper to taste

1. Chop the onion finely. Melt the margarine in a saucepan and sauté the onion for about 3 minutes.
2. Chop the tomato and add it to the pan. Cook for a further 2-3 minutes.
3. Drain the beans and put them into a bowl. Mash them coarsely (a potato masher or pastry blender is useful for this), leaving some of the beans whole.
4. Add the beans to the saucepan, stirring well. Season to taste, cook for a minute or two, then remove from heat. Turn into a shallow bowl, leave to cool then chill in refrigerator. Spread on toast, crispbread, or in sandwiches.

Week 5

SHOPPING LIST

Vegetables and Fruit

9 small onions
Parsley
Seasonal vegetables (for Sunday
    dinner)
2 oz (55g) mushrooms
1 small banana
Lettuce
Other salad ingredients
1 small carrot
Garlic
6-7 oz (170-200g) potatoes

Miscellaneous

15½ oz (440g) tin (can) tomatoes
2 oz (55g) walnuts
2 oz (55g) ground almonds
Miso
Brown rice flour
Coconut-flavoured soya (soy) milk
Cornflour (cornstarch)
Millet
15½ oz (440g) tin (can) borlotti (pinto)
    beans
Rolled oats
Soya (soy) flour
Baking powder
1 oz (30g)/1¾ tablespoons cashews
Smokey Snaps (imitation bacon bits)
Soya (soy) mayonnaise
Mango chutney
1 oz (30g)/1¾ tablespoons peanuts

Check that you have all the staples listed on page 13

SUNDAY LUNCH

Tomato Soup

Imperial (Metric)

1 small onion*
1 tablespoon vegetable oil*
7 oz (200g) tinned tomatoes*
½ teaspoon yeast extract*
½ teaspoon marjoram*
½ teaspoon basil*
¼ pint (140ml) water*
Sea salt and freshly ground black
　pepper to taste*
1 tablespoon minced parsley

American

1 small onion*
1 tablespoon vegetable oil*
7 ounces canned tomatoes*
½ teaspoon yeast extract*
½ teaspoon marjoram*
½ teaspoon sweet basil*
⅔ cup water*
Sea salt and freshly ground black
　pepper to taste*
1 tablespoon minced parsley

1. Chop the onion. Sauté in the oil for about 3 minutes.
2. Add the tomatoes, chopping them with a spoon while doing so. Add the yeast extract and herbs, bring to the boil, then lower heat and simmer, uncovered, for about 10 minutes.
3. Put the water and about half the soup mixture into a liquidizer and blend thoroughly. Return to saucepan, add seasoning, bring to the boil, then simmer for another minute or two.
4. Serve topped with minced parsley.

*If making the whole week's menus, use a large tin (can) of tomatoes and double all the starred ingredients; cool the half of the soup not eaten and then refrigerate for later use.

SUNDAY DINNER

Savoury Nut Pudding

Imperial (Metric)

1 small onion*
1 tablespoon vegetable oil*
1 tablespoon wholemeal flour*
⅛ pint (70ml) water*
1 oz (30g) walnuts*
1 oz (30g) ground almonds*
1 oz (30g) wholemeal breadcrumbs*
½ teaspoon sage*
½ teaspoon marjoram*
¼ teaspoon thyme*
1 tablespoon soya sauce*
Sea salt and freshly ground black
  pepper to taste*
Seasonal vegetables

American

1 small onion*
1 tablespoon vegetable oil*
1 tablespoon whole wheat flour*
⅓ cup water*
¼ cup walnuts*
¼ cup ground almonds*
½ cup fresh whole wheat
  breadcrumbs*
½ teaspoon sage*
½ teaspoon marjoram*
¼ teaspoon thyme*
1 tablespoon soy sauce*
Sea salt and freshly ground black
  pepper to taste*
Seasonal vegetables

1. Chop the onion and sauté in the oil in a pan for about 3 minutes. Stir in the flour and then the water, heating until it thickens and boils. Remove the pan from the heat.
2. Grind the walnuts. Add them to the pan, as well as the ground almonds, breadcrumbs, herbs, soya (soy) sauce and seasoning. Mix well.
3. Turn the mixture into a pudding basin, cover with foil, and place in a large pan of simmering water; cover the pan, and steam the dish for about 1½ hours. Serve with cooked seasonal vegetables and with Mushroom-miso Gravy (see right).

*If making the whole week's menus double all of these ingredients and make double the quantity of the dish; cool and then refrigerate half.

Mushroom-miso Gravy

Imperial (Metric)

1 oz (30g) mushrooms
2 teaspoons vegetable oil
⅛ pint (70ml) warm water
1 teaspoon miso
½ tablespoon brown rice flour

American

½ cup mushrooms
2 teaspoons vegetable oil
⅓ cup warm water
1 teaspoon miso
½ tablespoon brown rice flour

1. Chop the mushrooms. Sauté them in a small saucepan in the oil until tender.
2. Put the warm water, miso and rice flour into a liquidizer. Blend thoroughly.
3. Pour the mixture onto the mushrooms and stir well, over a low heat, until the gravy thickens.

SUNDAY DESSERT

Tropical Blancmange

Imperial (Metric)

¼ pint (140ml) plus 2 tablespoons
  coconut-flavoured soya milk
3 teaspoons cornflour
1 small banana

American

⅔ cup plus 2 tablespoons
  coconut-flavoured soymilk
3 teaspoons cornstarch
1 small banana

1. Heat the ¼ pint (140ml)/⅔ cup milk in a saucepan. Meanwhile, mix the 2 tablespoons milk and the cornflour (cornstarch). When the milk is boiling pour it onto the cornflour (cornstarch) mixture, stir, then return the mixture to the saucepan, bring to the boil, stirring constantly, and boil for a minute or so.
2. Slice the banana into a dessert dish and pour the thickened milk on top. Leave to cool, then refrigerate until ready to eat.

MONDAY

Millet Chilli (Chili)

Imperial (Metric)	American
2 oz (55g) millet*	½ cup millet*
6 fl oz (170ml) water	¾ cup water
Pinch sea salt	Pinch sea salt
1 small onion	1 small onion
1 tablespoon vegetable oil	1 tablespoon vegetable oil
1 teaspoon ground cumin	1 teaspoon ground cumin
1 teaspoon oregano	1 teaspoon oregano
½ teaspoon garlic salt	½ teaspoon garlic salt
¼-⅛ teaspoon chilli powder	¼-⅛ teaspoon chili powder
½ x 15½ oz (440g) tin borlotti beans	½ x 15½ ounce can pinto beans
⅛ pint (70ml) water	⅓ cup water
1 tablespoon tomato purée	1 tablespoon tomato paste

1. Cover the millet with the water and a pinch of salt. Bring to the boil, then lower heat, cover and simmer for about 20 minutes, by which time the water should be absorbed and the millet tender.
2. Meanwhile, chop the onion and sauté it in the oil for about 3 minutes. Lower heat and add the cumin, oregano, garlic salt and chilli (chili) powder. Stir well for a minute or so.
3. Drain and rinse the beans. Add them to the saucepan and stir for a minute or so longer. Add the water and the tomato purée (paste). Raise heat, bring to the boil, then lower heat and simmer uncovered for about 5 minutes.
4. Add the cooked millet to the beans, stir well, and cook for a minute or two longer.

*If making the whole week's menus cook double this amount of millet in double the amount of water; cool and then refrigerate half.

TUESDAY

Nut Rissoles with Tomato Sauce

Imperial (Metric)	American
Rissoles	*Rissoles*
Savoury Nut Pudding from Sunday (page 114)	Savoury Nut Pudding from Sunday (page 114)
2 tablespoons wholemeal flour	2 tablespoons whole wheat flour
2 tablespoons rolled oats	2 tablespoons rolled oats
Vegetable oil as required	Vegetable oil as required
Salad ingredients	Salad ingredients
*Tomato Sauce**	*Tomato Sauce**
Tomato soup from Sunday (page 113)	Tomato soup from Sunday (page 113)
½ oz (15g) brown rice flour	⅛ cup brown rice flour
1 tablespoon tomato purée	1 tablespoon tomato paste

1. Mash the nut mixture in a bowl. Stir in the flour.
2. Spread the oats out on a plate. Form the nut mixture into three rissoles, and coat them well on both sides with the oats.
3. Heat a little oil in a frying pan (skillet) and fry the rissoles, turning them once, until nicely browned on both sides. Serve accompanied by a side salad and topped with tomato sauce.
4. To make the tomato sauce, pour the soup into a liquidizer and add the rice flour and tomato purée (paste). Blend thoroughly. Pour into a saucepan, and heat gently until it thickens and comes to the boil. Simmer for a couple of minutes. (If you have not made the whole week's menus a good store-bought wholefood tomato sauce could be used instead.)

*N.B. This will be twice as much as required for one meal; after making the sauce cool and then refrigerate half to be used on Thursday night.

WEDNESDAY

Vegetable Dumplings

Imperial (Metric)	American
2½-3 oz (70-85g) wholemeal bread	2½-3 ounces whole wheat bread
¼ pint (140ml) soya milk	⅔ cup soymilk
1 small onion	1 small onion
1½ tablespoons vegan margarine	1½ tablespoons vegan margarine
1 small carrot	1 small carrot
1 oz (30g) mushrooms	½ cup mushrooms
3 tablespoons wholemeal flour	3 tablespoons whole wheat flour
2 tablespoons soya flour	2 tablespoons soy flour
¼ teaspoon baking powder	¼ teaspoon baking powder
Sea salt and freshly ground black pepper to taste	Sea salt and freshly ground black pepper to taste
Good grate of nutmeg	Good grate of nutmeg
1-2 tablespoons autolized yeast flakes	1-2 tablespoons Good Tasting Yeast flakes or powder

1. Dice the bread. Put the diced bread into a bowl and pour the milk over it. Turn over a few times then leave to soak.
2. Chop the onion finely. Sauté in a small saucepan in 1 tablespoon of the margarine for a minute or two. Chop the carrot and mushrooms finely. Add them to the pan and sauté for another minute or two. Lower heat, cover pan and leave the vegetables to cook in their own juices for 5-10 minutes.
3. Knead the milky bread well. Add both flours, baking powder, seasoning and nutmeg. Mix well. Stir in the vegetables. Leave to cool briefly.
4. Bring to the boil a largish saucepan of lightly salted water. Put tablespoons of the dumpling mixture into the water one at a time until all are in. Boil gently, uncovered, for 15-20 minutes.
5. Melt the remaining ½ tablespoon margarine.
6. Drain the dumplings carefully in a colander. Transfer them to a bowl or plate, pour the melted margarine over them and then sprinkle with yeast.

THURSDAY

Millet and Cashew Patties with Tomato Sauce

Imperial (Metric)	*American*
1 small onion	1 small onion
1 tablespoon vegetable oil plus additional for frying	1 tablespoon vegetable oil plus additional for frying
2 oz (55g) millet, cooked	½ cup millet, cooked
1 oz (30g) cashews	¼ cup cashews
2 tablespoons autolized yeast flakes	2 tablespoons Good Tasting Yeast, flakes or powder
Sea salt and freshly ground black pepper to taste	Sea salt and freshly ground black pepper to taste
Tomato sauce (see Tuesday, page 118)	Tomato sauce (see Tuesday, page 118)
Salad ingredients	Salad ingredients

1. Chop the onion finely. Heat 1 tablespoon of the oil in a saucepan and sauté the onion for about 3 minutes.
2. Add the cooked millet to the pan and mash it well. Stir briefly, then remove from heat.
3. Grind the cashews. Add them to the millet, along with the yeast and seasoning. Mix well and form into 4 patties.
4. Fry the patties in a little oil in a frying pan until lightly browned on both sides. Serve topped with the remainder of Tuesday's tomato sauce which has been gently reheated (or use a proprietary brand tomato sauce), accompanied by a side salad.

FRIDAY

Pasta e Fagioli

Imperial (Metric)	American
6 oz (170g) wholemeal macaroni	6 ounces whole wheat macaroni
1 small onion	1 small onion
1 small clove garlic	1 small clove garlic
1 tablespoon olive oil	1 tablespoon olive oil
½ x 15½ oz (440g) tin borlotti beans	½ x 15½ ounce can pinto beans
1 tablespoon tomato purée	1 tablespoon tomato paste
2 tablespoons water	2 tablespoons water
1 teaspoon basil	1 teaspoon sweet basil
1 tablespoon minced parsley	1 tablespoon minced parsley
Freshly ground black pepper	Freshly ground black pepper
1 tablespoon Smokey Snaps	1 tablespoon imitation bacon bits

1. Cook the macaroni in boiling, lightly salted water until just tender.
2. Meanwhile, chop the onion and garlic finely. Sauté in the oil in a saucepan for about 3 minutes.
3. Add the beans, tomato purée (paste), water and basil. Bring to the boil, then lower heat and simmer, uncovered, for about 5 minutes.
4. Drain the macaroni and add it to the saucepan, along with the parsley, pepper to taste and Smokey Snaps (imitation bacon bits). Mix well and cook for a couple of minutes longer.

SATURDAY LUNCH

Curried Potato and Peanut Salad

Imperial (Metric)

6-7 oz (170-200g) potatoes
1 small onion
1 tablespoon vegetable oil
¼ teaspoon coriander
¼ teaspoon cumin
¼ teaspoon turmeric
¼ teaspoon powdered ginger
Pinch chilli powder
2 tablespoons soya mayonnaise
1 tablespoon mango chutney
1 oz (30g) peanuts
Sea salt and freshly ground black
  pepper to taste
Lettuce as required

American

6-7 ounces potatoes
1 small onion
1 tablespoon vegetable oil
¼ teaspoon coriander
¼ teaspoon cumin
¼ teaspoon turmeric
¼ teaspoon powdered ginger
Pinch chili powder
2 tablespoons soy mayonnaise
1 tablespoon mango chutney
1¾ tablespoons peanuts
Sea salt and freshly ground black
  pepper to taste
Lettuce as required

1. Cook the potatoes until tender. Drain and cool.
2. Chop the onion. Sauté it in the oil in a small saucepan until beginning to brown. Lower heat and add the spices; cook for a minute or so longer. Remove from heat and cool.
3. Chop the potatoes and add them to the saucepan. Stir in the mayonnaise, chutney and peanuts, and season to taste. Transfer to a bowl, chill thoroughly and serve on a bed of lettuce.

Index